A Taste of Lebanon
COOKING TODAY THE LEBANESE WAY

D0891191

Over 200 Recipes
developed and tested

by **Mary Salloum**

INTERLINK BOOKS
An Imprint of Interlink Publishing Group, Inc.
NEW YORK

First paperback edition published in 1992 by

Interlink Books
An imprint of Interlink Publishing Group, Inc.
99 Seventh Avenue
Brooklyn, New York 11215

Library of Congress Cataloging-in-Publication Data

Salloum, Mary.
   A taste of Lebanon.
   Includes index.
   1. Cookery, Lebanese. I. Title.
TX 725.L4S25   1988   641.595692   88-596
ISBN 0-940793-08-3 — ISBN 0-940793-90-3 (pbk.)   CIP

Photography by Commercial Illustrators Ltd.
Graphics by Concept One Design Ltd.
Printed and bound in Hong Kong

TO MY MOTHER

CONTENTS

INTRODUCTION

What's nutritious, delicious, inexpensive and fun to make? Lebanese food, of course! Many in the Western countries have only recently become familiar with this interesting and savory cuisine.

I was born in Lebanon and have enjoyed the Lebanese traditions all my life. Since moving to Canada, in 1952, I have been sharing my knowledge and enthusiasm for Lebanese cooking. The positive reaction I have received has prompted me to write this book and make it possible for everyone to enjoy a taste of Lebanon.

Health food enthusiasts, vegetarians and anyone who loves delicious foods will welcome these step-by-step instructions for the preparation of Lebanese cuisine.

Cooking today the Lebanese way means creating sophisticated Lebanese foods with Western touches. A little imagination, lots of herbs and spices and a variety of inexpensive ingredients, produce unusual and tasty results. Preparation of some menus are time consuming, while others require only minutes to make.

Every Lebanese daughter will claim that her mother is the best cook, and I am no exception. The recipes in this book have been handed down from mother to daughter for generations with "a pinch of this and a handful of that" as the only guidelines. Now you can enjoy a Taste of Lebanon made to measure; the gateway is open for a delicious food experience.

"Sahtayn!" To your good health!

Mary Salloum

Mary Salloum

"It is the spirit that hovers over Lebanon,
conversing with kings and prophets,
singing with the rivers the songs of Solomon,
and repeating with the Holy Cedars of Lebanon
the memory of ancient glory. "

Kahlil Gibran

Grateful acknowledgement

to Citadel Press, Inc., New Jersey, U.S.A.
For permission to use the quotation by Kahlil Gibran taken
from *The Treasured Writings of Kahlil Gibran.*

ABOUT LEBANON

Lebanon, the land of the Phoenicians, is the Gateway to the Middle East with its famed cedars and distinctive culture. This country, a mere 156 miles in length and 31 miles in width, has offered to the world not only many great products and customs, but also the origin of the Phonetic Alphabet. Its people, though contained in such a small area, can vary greatly in their way of life. Traces of old-fashioned methods and practices are still found in the many villages situated within this country while the cities display progressive urbanization – highrises, exquisite restaurants and formal education institutions like the American University of Beirut.

Though differences do exist in terms of lifestyles, the Lebanese culture is always distinctive. There may be a slight variation in menu and recipes from town to town, but the basic dishes remain the same and can be found in any city restaurant. Also, all regions of Lebanon exhibit the unmistakable Lebanese trait of hospitality. A Lebanese household will insistently offer a guest, be he friend, family or stranger, a variety of homemade dishes and may even regard a refusal to eat as an insult.

Lebanon is bordered on the north and east by Syria, on the south by Israel and on the west by the beautiful Mediterranean Sea. One may snow ski in the mountains in the morning and waterski in the Mediterranean in the afternoon. The scenery is truly magnificent with a blend of the ancient in Byblos and Tyre, the ultra-modern in Beirut and the breath-taking in valleys such as Besharre, the birthplace of Kahlil Gibran.

The natural and nutritious food of Lebanon is made from the country's own produce. Grains, vegetables, nuts and luscious fruits including pomegranates grow for all to enjoy. Olive groves offer not only the olives that are always kept on the table for a snack or for breakfast, but also the olive oil which is used in all salads and appetizers. Grapes grow in abundance, and the vineyards are essential for making wine and Arak, a Lebanese liquor.

The Lebanese home is stocked with yogurt, cheese, olives, nuts and grains, and the Lebanese cook may spend many hours in the kitchen preparing a selection of dishes. Often, she adjusts her cooking to meet the individual tastes of each family member.

Lebanon – the land of the Cedars of the Lord looks down from the mountains to the sea below. Here the archaic and metropolitan blend to form a beautiful and proud land.

BASIC INGREDIENTS FOR
LEBANESE COOKING

BURGHUL   – (crushed wheat) sometimes referred to as bulgar.

KISHK   – Is a powdered soup base made from fermented burghul and yogurt.

MAHLAB   – Is derived from black-cherry kernels. A spice ground into a powder.

PINE NUTS   – A nut found in a cone in some pine trees.

ROSE WATER – A liquid extracted from rose petals.

SUMAC   – Clusters of berries that turn to a crimson color. Only the outside skin of the berry is used. A tart taste, similar to lemon flavor.

TAHINI   – (Sesame Seed Paste) – crushed sesame seeds, made into a paste.

ZAHTAR   – Is a blend of thyme, sumac and summer savory.

These ingredients may be purchased in grocery import outlets, Middle Eastern grocery stores, health food stores, delicatessens and the import section in some super-markets.

CHICK PEAS   – (Garbanzos)

LENTILS

OLIVE OIL

YOGURT

These ingredients may be found in most super markets.

HELPFUL HINTS

- Dry Chick Peas (Garbanzo Beans) or any dry beans may be soaked overnight, drained, placed in plastic bags and frozen to use at a later time. Soak 1 - 2 pounds at a time, use as required. Note that the recipe may ask for dry peas or beans. After soaking, beans will double in volume. Therefore if a ½ cup dry is called for then use 1 cup soaked.

- For an added flavor in soups, place ½-1 cup of the frozen peas or beans directly into the soup while cooking.

- After baking or barbequing an eggplant with the skin on, run it under cold water first to make the skin easier to remove.

- Eggplant should be placed in cold, salted water after peeling and slicing to prevent discoloring.

- Lamb meat in Lebanon is plentiful. Beef or lamb may be used in the recipes in this book. It is best to carve your own meat and clean it properly using a leg of lamb or a roast of beef. This especially applies to Kibbi dishes when only the leanest meat is used.

- Fish should always be salted for 1 hour before cooking. Always remove the eyes when cooking a whole fish. (Before frying fish, leave at room temperature for a few minutes).

- Burghul recipes in this book are for either fine or coarse. Fine burghul is specified as "burghul" in the recipes. When coarse burghul is used in a recipe it is defined as "coarse crushed wheat".

- If there is left over Kibbi Nayii, dampen hands with water and mix until pliable. Form into Kibbi balls or patties and fry. Kibbi balls may also be frozen and used at a later date to add to soup.

- Yogurt is one of the staple foods in the Lebanese home. Always save a small amount of starter for the next time you wish to make it.

- When cooking yogurt, stir constantly in one direction to avoid curdling and scorching.

- Butter should be brought to a boil for 5 minutes over low heat to remove the salt and water. Skim off the foam and save to use in rice fillings and for frying vegetables. Carefully pour butter into a container (not plastic), and discard residue left in the bottom of the pan. Unsalted or clarified butter may be used in place of regular salted butter for cooking.

- Syrup (Atter) should be cold when poured over warm pastries and desserts for better results, but if the pastry is cold, then the syrup should be warm.

- Lemon juice should be fresh for salads, although concentrated may be used.

- Herbs and spices are of great importance in Lebanese cooking. Many home-makers dry their own herbs to be used in the winter months. Cinnamon is always sprinkled in tomato sauce and vegetable fillings. What is yogurt without the mint? A salad without the parsley and garlic?

- Lebanese foods are very convenient to have as left overs. They store very well for several days in the refrigerator. Warm before serving if necessary.

- Meat Reserve (Awarma) may be substituted for ground meat in stews. The oil or butter used for browning the meat may be omitted, as the fat from the Awarma is sufficient.

- Use a little Awarma when frying eggs or vegetables. Warm the Awarma in the pan then add the other ingredients.

MEASURING TERMS USED IN THIS BOOK

tsp – Teaspoon
Tbsp – Tablespoon

An 8 ounce cup is the same as 250 mL
2 inches is about 5 cm
2 pounds is a little less than 1 kg
1 pound is a little less than 500 g
325°F oven temperature for roasting

OVEN TEMPERATURE GUIDE

140°F –	60°C		375°F –	190°C
150°F –	70°C		400°F –	200°C
170°F –	80°C		425°F –	220°C
200°F –	100°C		450°F –	230°C
250°F –	120°C		475°F –	240°C
275°F –	140°C		500°F –	260°C
300°F –	150°C		525°F –	270°C
325°F –	160°C		550°F –	290°C
350°F –	180°C			

Appetizers and Sauces
(Mezza)

The Lebanese view the before dinner period as a time of relaxation and friendly conversation. A game of backgammon is usually in progress, and Arak, an anise flavored liquor, is often enjoyed.

Before dinner is served, a selection of hors d'oeuvres is nibbled on for sometimes two to three hours. Mezza dishes are made up of pickles, yogurt, cheese, sauces, fish dishes, Kibbi, salads, cooked and raw meats and vegetables.

Sesame Seed Paste (Tahini) makes a very tasty sauce or dip and is used quite frequently in salads and cooked vegetables. This type of Mezza could very well replace a full course meal.

Lebanese cuisine will truly leave one in awe, as anywhere between twenty to sixty or more elaborate dishes are placed on the table — and this is only the beginning of Lebanese hospitality!

From the Top, Down — *Kidney Salad, Chick Pea Dip, Broad Beans in Lemon, Eggplant Appetizer, Mushroom Salad*

Kidney Salad

Salatet Kalawi

2 lbs. beef or lamb kidney
1 clove garlic
1 tsp. salt
¼ tsp. pepper

3 Tbsp. olive oil
3 Tbsp. lemon juice
1 tsp. coriander
¼ cup parsley (finely chopped)

Wash kidney well, removing all fat tissue. Place kidney in pot; cover with water and add a sprinkle of salt. Cook until tender. Drain, rinse and cool. Cut into bite size pieces; set aside.

In a salad bowl crush garlic and salt. Add pepper, oil, lemon juice, and coriander. Blend well. Add kidney pieces and parsley, mixing well.

Refrigerate for 1 - 2 hours. Toss lightly before serving.

Chick Pea Dip

Hommous bi Tahini   Meatless

This is the most popular of dips in the Middle East with a most delightful tangy flavor.

1 19 oz. can chick peas or garbanzo beans (drain liquid and save)
¼ cup Sesame Seed Paste (Tahini)
1 clove garlic
½ tsp. salt
¼ cup lemon juice (or to taste)

Combine all above ingredients in a food processor or blender, adding only enough of the saved liquid to meet your satisfaction (the more liquid added, the thinner the dip). Blend for 2 - 3 minutes to a smooth paste. Place in a small platter or shallow bowl. If preferred, sprinkle olive oil on top and garnish with parsley sprigs and lemon wedges.

To serve: Tear off pieces of Pita Bread or cut Pita into wedges and dip into Hommous.

Serve with any fish recipe, Baked Kibbi (page 102), Tabouli (page 43), Barbequed Chicken (page 83), or Shish Kabob (page 51).

Eggplant Appetizer

Baba Ghannuj

Every Appetizer (Mezza) table must have Baba Ghannuj.

1 large eggplant
1 clove garlic (crushed)
1 tsp. salt
¼ cup Sesame Seed Paste (Tahini)
2 Tbsp. water

¼ cup lemon juice
lemon wedges
parsley
olive oil

Set oven at 375°F. Wash eggplant and remove stem. Pierce with a fork 4 -6 times. Place in baking dish. Bake for 45 minutes or until tender. Remove from oven and run under cold water. Peel and mash; set aside.

In serving bowl combine garlic, salt and Sesame Seed Paste. Gradually add water and lemon juice, beating well. Fold in mashed eggplant. Garnish with lemon wedges, finely chopped parsley and a sprinkle of olive oil.

Scoop up eggplant with pieces of Pita Bread to eat or serve as a side dish with any meal.

Broad Beans in Lemon

Fool m'Dammas

A very popular dish in the Middle East.

2 cups dried fava beans or broad beans
  (soaked overnight)
2 cloves garlic (crushed)
1 tsp. salt
½ cup lemon juice

¼ cup olive oil
½ cup parsley (finely chopped)
green onions
lemon wedges

Drain beans and place in saucepan. Cover with water. Cover pan with lid and simmer until tender (approximately 1 hour). If too much water evaporates during the cooking period, add ½ - 1 cup to prevent sticking. Beans should be covered.

In serving bowl combine garlic, salt and lemon juice; mix well.

Mash beans and some of the liquid. Mix thoroughly, and add garlic mixture. Sprinkle oil over top of beans. Garnish with chopped parsley, green onions and lemon wedges. Serve hot or cold.

May be served for breakfast or lunch with Pita Bread.

Mushroom Salad
Salatet Futter

1 clove garlic (crushed)
1 lb. whole mushrooms (fresh or canned)
1 medium onion (sliced in rings)
1 medium green pepper (sliced in strips)
¼ cup chopped parsley

1 tsp. salt
¼ tsp. pepper
¼ cup lemon juice
¼ cup olive oil

Combine all ingredients in a salad bowl. Toss well. May be kept in refrigerator for 1-2 hours to marinate. Serve chilled.

Tongue Salad
Salatet Lisaan

1 beef or 3 lamb tongue
2 cloves garlic (crushed)
½ tsp. salt
¼ cup lemon juice
1 tsp. basil

¼ cup olive oil
¼ tsp. pepper
½ cup parsley (finely chopped)
2 green onions (finely chopped)

Cook tongue in a pot of water with a pinch of salt until tender (beef tongue will require a longer period of cooking, about 1 hour).

Remove from water and let cool. Peel off skin. Chop into bite sizes pieces and set aside.

In serving bowl combine garlic, salt, lemon juice, basil, oil and pepper. Blend well. Add tongue pieces, parsley and onions; toss well. If preferred, salad may be left to marinate in refrigerator for 1-2 hours before serving.

Liver Salad
Salatet Kibdy

2 lbs. liver (calf or lamb)
1 small onion (sliced in thin rings)
¼ cup parsley (finely chopped)
3 Tbsp. olive oil
3 Tbsp. lemon juice

1 clove garlic (crushed)
1 tsp. salt
¼ tsp. pepper
1 tsp. basil

Set oven at 500°F. Place liver on greased cookie sheet. Bake for 15 minutes or until liver is cooked, turning once. Let cool. Chop into bite size pieces; set aside.

In a salad bowl combine all remaining ingredients; mix well. Add the liver and toss. Serve immediately or place in refrigerator to marinate for 1-2 hours.

Falafil

Frequently found in restaurants and delicatessans. For a quick lunch, Falafil is also sold by street vendors as hot dogs are sold in the Western countries.

1 lb. chick peas
  (soaked for 24 hours)
1 medium onion
1 medium potato (peeled)
4 cloves garlic
1 tsp. coriander (ground)
1 tsp. cumin

2 tsp. salt (or to taste)
½ tsp. pepper
½ tsp. cayenne (or to taste)
1 Tbsp. flour
  vegetable oil for frying
1 recipe Sesame Seed Sauce (page 26)
2 tsp. baking soda

Drain chick peas. Quarter onion and potato. Run all through fine holes of the meat grinder along with the garlic two times.

Add all remaining ingredients except baking soda, vegetable oil and Sesame Seed Sauce. Mix well. Run through grinder once more. Mix again. Cover and leave to rest for two to three hours.

Heat oil for deep frying. While oil is heating add baking soda to the chick pea mixture. With dampened hands, form mixture into balls the size of a walnut, then flatten slightly into a pattie. Deep fry, making sure patties are cooked through and are golden brown. Remove from oil with a slotted spoon and drain on paper towels.

Serve 3 or 4 patties inside a loaf of Pita Bread by opening bread around the outside edges of the round, leaving approximately 3 inches intact. Add sliced radishes, chopped parsley, diced tomatoes, pickles and hot peppers. Drizzle Sesame Seed Sauce over the vegetables.

Bring the top layer of Pita over to cover the filling. Roll, starting from one side, or cut a small Pita Bread in half to form a pocket and fill. Patties may also be served without the Pita Bread, by dipping them into the Sesame Seed Sauce.

VARIATION:
(1) ½ lb. dry fava beans or dry broad beans and ½ lb. chick peas may be used, following the same directions.
(2) A food processor may be used in place of a meat grinder.

Meatball Appetizers

Zonkol Laham

1 lb. lean beef or lamb (ground)
¼ cup parsley (finely chopped)
1 small onion (finely grated)
¼ tsp. cumin

1 tsp. salt
¼ tsp. pepper
¼ tsp. cayenne

Place all ingredients in a mixing bowl. Mix well. Heat oven to 400 °F. Form small balls the size of marbles and place them on a cookie sheet. Bake for approximately 10-15 minutes or until cooked through.

Serve hot on toothpicks.

VARIATION:
Meatballs may be dipped into Sesame Seed Sauce (page 26) or Garlic Sauce (page 25).

Garlic Sauce

Tume bi Ziet   Meatless

4 cloves garlic
½ cup olive oil
¼ cup lemon juice

¼ tsp. salt
dash of cayenne

Blend all above ingredients in blender or food processor until garlic is mashed.

To serve: Dip cooked chicken or meat pieces, vegetables or Pita Bread into the sauce.

Walnut Sauce

Jauz bi Tahini   Meatless

2 cloves garlic   ½ tsp. salt
1 cup walnut pieces   ¼ tsp. cayenne
1 Tbsp. Sesame Seed Paste (Tahini)   ¼ cup water
¼ cup lemon juice

Place all above ingredients in a blender or food processor. Blend for 2 minutes. Sauce may be served a little coarse but if one prefers a smoother texture, blend for another minute.

Sauce may be used for dipping raw vegetables, Pita Bread pieces, or for fish dishes.

Sesame Seed Sauce

Taratour   Meatless

1 clove garlic   ½ cup cold water
½ tsp. salt   ½ cup lemon juice
½ cup Sesame Seed Paste (Tahini)

Crush garlic and salt together in mixing bowl. Blend in Sesame Seed Paste. Gradually add water, blending well. Then, blend in lemon juice until smooth. If a thicker sauce is preferred, use less water.

Serve with Fried Cauliflower (page 115), Fried Eggplant (page 114), fried potatoes and fish dishes. Use as a dip for breads or raw vegetables, or as a dressing for any raw or cooked vegetable salad.

VARIATION:
All ingredients may be placed in blender or food processor and blended for 1 minute.

Pine Nut Sauce

Snoobar bi Limoon   Meatless

1 cup pine nuts
2 cloves garlic
¼ tsp. salt

1 cup lemon juice
dash of cayenne
parsley

Combine all ingredients, except parsley, in a blender or food processor, and blend to a smooth paste.

Serve with any fish recipe, use as a dip for fresh vegetables, or a dip for Pita Bread. Garnish with chopped parsley.

Parsley in Tahini Sauce

Bakdunis bi Taratour   Meatless

1 clove garlic
½ tsp. salt
½ cup Sesame Seed Paste (Tahini)
½ cup water

½ cup lemon juice
¼ tsp. cayenne
½ cup parsley (finely chopped)

Mash garlic and salt together in a bowl. Add Tahini, blending well (Tahini will thicken). Gradually add water to soften mixture. Blend in lemon juice and cayenne, then stir in parsley.

Serve as a dip for fresh vegetables, fish, as a dip for Pita Bread, or Barbequed Chicken (page 83).

VARIATION:
Blend all ingredients, except parsley, in a blender or food processor until smooth. Stir in parsley.

Soups

Hearty Lebanese soups may be made with meats, legumes, beans and vegetables. They may even be served as a main dish with a variety of other accompaniments.

A favorite Lebanese soup is called Kishk. To make kishk, yogurt and crushed wheat (burghul) are fermented together for several days. This mixture is then dried and ground into a fine powder to be used as the soup base.* This dish may be served hot accompanied by pieces of Pita Bread.

Lentils are a common ingredient in Lebanese soups. Lentils, like beans, are rich in protein.

Lebanese soups keep well under refrigeration; they may be reheated and retain their full flavor.

*It is available at most specialty stores.

Top — *Lentil Soup*
Bottom — *Chicken Chick Pea Soup*

Lentil Soup

Shourabit Adas

1 cup ground beef or lamb	1 cup swiss chard stalks, chopped
1 large onion (coarsely chopped)	(optional)
2 Tbsp. butter	salt and pepper to taste
1½ cups lentils	1 lemon, cut in half
10 cups water	

Sauté meat, onions and butter in large saucepan. When meat is brown, add lentils, water, swiss chard, salt and pepper. Cover and cook until lentils are tender.

Serve with a squeeze of lemon juice.

VARIATION:
Split lentils may be substituted for whole lentils.

Chicken-Chick Pea Soup

Shourabit Djaj mah Hommous

½ chicken (cut up)	2 tsp. salt (or to taste)
10 cups water	½ tsp. pepper
¾ cup dry chick peas (soaked overnight)	¼ tsp. cinnamon
½ cup rice (washed and drained)	

Clean chicken pieces and place in large saucepan with the water. When chicken comes to a boil, skim off the foam. Add drained chick peas. Cover and cook for 45 minutes over medium heat.

Add rice, salt, pepper and cinnamon. Cook an additional 25 minutes.

Serve.

Lentil and Bean Soup

Shourabit Adas mah Fasoolia   Meatless

¼ cup chick peas (soaked overnight)   1 large onion (coarsely chopped)
¼ cup lima beans (soaked overnight)   ½ cup vegetable oil
¼ cup kidney beans   ¼ cup rice
   (soaked overnight)   ½ tsp. cumin
¼ cup lentils (washed and drained)   salt and pepper to taste
10 cups water

Place drained peas, beans and lentils in a saucepan with water. Bring to a boil over high heat. Lower heat, cover and cook for approximately 45 minutes.

Sauté onion in oil until golden brown and add to bean mixture. Add rice, cumin, salt and pepper. Continue to cook for an additional 30 minutes.

Serve.

Spinach Soup

Shourabit Sabanikh

1 lb. stew meat (beef or lamb)   2 tsp. salt (or to taste)
¼ cup butter   ¼ tsp. pepper
1 large onion (coarsely diced)   ¼ tsp. cinnamon
3 cloves garlic (crushed)   2 lbs. spinach (finely chopped)
10 cups water   ¼ cup parsley (finely chopped)
½ cup rice (washed and drained)

Place meat and butter in large saucepan. Sauté until meat is browned. Add onions and garlic. Sauté until onion is transparent. Add water and cook until mixture comes to a boil. Cover and cook over medium heat until meat is tender.

Add rice and cook for 20 minutes, then add seasonings and spinach. Bring to boil again and cook for an additional 10 minutes. Add parsley, stir and serve.

Split Lentil Soup

Adas Majroush   Meatless

1½ cups split lentils
8-9 cups water
¼ cup rice (washed and drained)
1 medium onion (finely chopped)

⅓ cup vegetable oil
1½ tsp. salt (or to taste)
¼ tsp. pepper
1 lemon, cut in half

Combine lentils and water in saucepan. Bring to boil over high heat. Lower heat to medium, cover and cook lentils at a steady boil for 45 minutes or until tender.

Stir in rice and continue cooking.

In a small skillet, sauté onion in oil until lightly browned. Add to lentil mixture. Add salt and pepper and stir. Turn heat to low and cook for 30 minutes, stirring occasionally to prevent sticking.

Serve with a squeeze of lemon juice on each serving.

Shank Soup

Shourabit el Mouzat

2 lamb or beef shanks
1 cinnamon stick
10 cups water
3 large tomatoes (diced small)

1 small onion (coarsely chopped)
½ cup rice
½ cup parsley (coarsely chopped)
salt and pepper to taste

Place shanks and cinnamon stick in a large saucepan with the water. Bring to a boil over high heat. Skim off foam. Lower heat to medium. Cover and cook until meat is tender (approximately 1 hour).

Add tomatoes, onion and rice. Cover and cook for an additional 25 minutes.

Add parsley, salt and pepper. Serve.

Mixed Soup

Shouraba Makhluta

1 lb. lamb or beef (cut into 1 inch cubes)   10 cups water
1 medium onion (quartered)   2 tsp. salt
1 cinnamon stick   ¼ tsp. pepper
1½ cups mixed dry legumes

Place all ingredients in a large saucepan. Bring to a boil. Lower heat, cover and cook for 1 hour or until legumes are tender.

Serve.

VARIATION:
1 cup diced potatoes or sliced carrots may be added during the last 30 minutes of cooking.

Potato-Lentil Soup

Shourabit Batata mah Adas

1 lb. beef or lamb (ground)   10 cups water
1 medium onion (coarsely chopped)   3 medium potatoes (diced small)
3 Tbsp. vegetable oil   1½ tsp. salt (or to taste)
1 cup lentils (washed and drained)   ¼ tsp. pepper

Sauté meat and onion in oil in a large saucepan until meat changes color. Add lentils and water. Cover and cook until lentils are tender (approximately 45 minutes).

Add potatoes, salt and pepper. Cook until potatoes are tender.

Serve with Pita Bread pieces – either fresh or crisp bread is suitable.

Chicken-Rice Soup

Shourabit Djaj

½ **chicken (cut up)**	**salt and pepper to taste**
10 cups water	**cinnamon**
1 **cup rice (washed and drained)**	

Wash and clean chicken pieces and place in large saucepan with the water. Bring to a boil over high heat. Skim off the foam. Cover and cook over medium heat for 60 minutes.

Remove chicken from liquid and debone. Return chicken to liquid. Add rice, salt and pepper. Cook for 25 minutes.

Serve with crisp Pita Bread pieces dropped into the soup. Add a sprinkle of cinnamon to each serving.

Kishk Soup

Shourabit Kishk

Kishk may be found in Middle Eastern stores. It is made with crushed wheat and yogurt, and rubbed into a fine powder.

½ **cup beef or lamb (finely diced)** *or*	1 **cup kishk**
½ **cup meat reserve (Awarma – page 62)**	**4-5 cups water**
1 **small onion (finely chopped)**	**salt to taste**
2 **cloves garlic (finely chopped)**	

Combine meat, onion and garlic in saucepan. Sauté over medium heat until onion is transparent. Stir in kishk. Blend in water. Bring to boil over medium heat, stirring occasionally. Add salt. Lower heat and simmer for 10-15 minutes.

Serve with pieces of Pita Bread.

Delicious served with left over cold Lentils with Rice (Moujadara – page 116) added to the soup.

VARIATION:
Peel and dice a large potato into small pieces. Saute with the meat, onion and garlic, following the same directions as above.

Vegetable Soup

Shourabit el Khodra

1-2 beef or lamb shanks
10 cups water
1 cinnamon stick
2 fresh tomatoes (diced small)
1 cup turnips (diced small)
1 cup carrots (diced small)

1½ cups fresh green beans
¼ cup rice
¼ cup tomato paste
salt and pepper to taste
1½ Tbsp. parsley (finely chopped)

Place shanks and water in a large saucepan, boil for 5 minutes. Skim off the foam. Turn heat to medium, cover and cook for 1 hour, or until tender.

Add cinnamon stick, tomatoes, turnips and carrots. Cut beans into 1½ inch pieces and add them to the mixture. Add the rice.

Cover and cook for 25-30 minutes on medium heat. Add tomato paste, salt and pepper. Cook for another 10 minutes. Remove from heat, add parsley.

Serve.

Chicken-Vegetable Soup

Shourabit Djaj mah Khodra

1 lb. chicken backs and necks
9-10 cups water
½ cup rice (washed and drained)
1 cup carrots (diced small)
1 cup potatoes (diced small)

1 cup peas (fresh or frozen)
1½ tsp. salt (or to taste)
¼ tsp. cinnamon
¼ tsp. pepper

Place chicken backs and necks and the water in a large saucepan. Boil for 5 minutes. Skim off foam.

Turn heat to medium, cover and cook for 30 minutes.

Add rice, vegetables and seasonings. Cover and cook for another 30 minutes.

Serve with Pita Bread pieces dropped into each serving, and a sprinkle of cinnamon on top.

Meatball Soup

Shourabit Laham Mizankal

1 small onion (grated)	¼ cup butter
1 tsp. salt	8-10 cups water
¼ tsp. pepper	1 cinnamon stick
¼ tsp. allspice	½ cup rice (washed and drained)
1 lb. ground beef or lamb	salt to taste
¼ cup parsley (finely chopped)	cinnamon

Place onions, salt, pepper and allspice in mixing bowl. Mix, working the seasonings into the onions. Add meat and parsley. Mix well. Form mixture into balls the size of a walnut.

In a skillet, brown meatballs in the butter. Add a ½ cup of the water. Place meatballs and stock in a large saucepan. Add cinnamon stick and remaining water. Boil for 10-15 minutes.

Add rice and salt to taste. Cook for an additional 30 minutes.

Serve with a dash of cinnamon on top.

Tomato Soup

Shourabit el Banadoora

1 or 2 beef or lamb shanks	2 Tbsp. tomato paste
1 cinnamon stick	½ cup rice (washed and drained)
7 cups water	salt, pepper and cinnamon
6 medium tomatoes	to taste

In large saucepan place shanks, cinnamon stick and water. Boil for 5 minutes. Skim off foam. Lower heat to medium, cover and cook for 1 hour.

While shanks are cooking, quarter tomatoes and place in another saucepan. Cook on low heat, cover and simmer until soft then strain them.

When shanks are tender, add the strained tomatoes, tomato paste, rice and seasonings. Cook for 30 minutes on low heat.

Salads

A Lebanese meal is not complete without a salad. Fresh parsley and mint are always added for a distinctive flavor. The Queen of Lebanese salads is Tabouli, made with parsley and burghul. Romaine lettuce is used to scoop up the Tabouli for eating.

One flavorful dressing used in Lebanese salads is made with garlic, olive oil and fresh lemon juice. Another dressing, using Sesame Seed Paste (Tahini), lemon juice and garlic, is a welcome change for a tangy flavor.

A popular salad served for lunches and snacks is Fatoosh, made with crisp pieces of Pita Bread. And yet another healthy and delicious salad, made with Romaine lettuce, is the traditional Lebanese Salad. This crisp salad, using the olive oil dressing, is the most popular in Lebanese cooking.

Cooked vegetables also make for a marvelous salad. With the added dressings, a salad is no longer just a salad.

Top — *Bean Salad*
Centre — *Lebanese Salad*
Bottom — *Bread Salad*

Bean Salad

Salatet Fasoolia

1-19 oz. can kidney beans
1-19 oz. can chick peas
1-19 oz. can lima beans

¼ cup parsley (finely chopped)
1 small red onion (sliced in rings)
1 Lebanese Salad dressing recipe (page 42)

Rinse all beans in cold water. Drain and place in salad bowl. Add parsley and onion rings. Drizzle salad dressing over the beans. Toss gently. This salad may be placed in the refrigerator to marinate for 1-2 hours for added flavor, or served immediately.

Serve with Lamb with Burghul (page 106) or Fried Vegetables.

Lebanese Salad

Salata Libnaniya

8 leaves of Romaine lettuce
4 green onions (coarsely chopped)
3 tomatoes (cubed)
1 English cucumber (sliced)

¼ cup parsley (finely chopped)
¼ cup fresh mint (chopped) or
2 Tbsp. dry mint
1 Lebanese Salad dressing recipe (page 42)

Wash and drain lettuce leaves and tear into bite size pieces. Place in salad bowl and add remaining ingredients. Add previously mixed salad dressing. Toss and serve immediately.

Serve with Lentils with Rice (page 116), Kibbi Nayii (page 103), or Burghul Pilaf (page 107).

Bread Salad

Fatoosh

2 small Pita Bread (whole)
8 Romaine lettuce leaves
1 bunch radishes (sliced)
2 green onions (chopped)
1 cucumber (sliced)
3 medium tomatoes (cut into wedges)
¼ cup parlsey (finely chopped)
1 clove garlic (crushed) optional

2 Tbsp. sumac herb (optional)
¼ cup lemon juice (or to taste)
¼ cup olive oil
1 tsp. salt
¼ tsp. pepper
¼ cup fresh mint (chopped)
  or
2 Tbsp. dry mint

Place the Pita Bread in oven to crisp. Break up into bite size pieces and place in large salad bowl. Wash and drain lettuce. Tear into bite size pieces and add to bread. Add all remaining ingredients; toss well.

Serve as a light snack or for lunch.

Lebanese Salad Dressing

Mtabbel la Salata

1 clove garlic
1 tsp. salt
¼ tsp. pepper

¼ cup lemon juice
¼ cup olive oil (or good quality
  vegetable oil)

In a small mixing bowl, crush garlic and salt together. Add pepper, lemon juice and oil, blending well. May be used over any salad or vegetables.

Tabouli

The Queen of Lebanese Salads. You may never want a plain salad again!

3 large bunches of parsley	2 large tomatoes (diced small)
1/3 cup crushed wheat (burghul)	1 1/2 tsp. salt
2 cups water	1/4 tsp. pepper
4 green onions, with ends	1/3 cup lemon juice (or to taste)
1/4 cup fresh mint (chopped) *or*	1/4 cup olive oil or vegetable oil
2 Tbsp. dry	

Wash parsley well, drain and shake out excess moisture.

Soak crushed wheat in water in a large mixing bowl for 2 minutes. Drain well. Set aside while preparing other ingredients.

Remove stems from parsley and discard. Chop parsley very fine (3 bunches should equal 5 cups). Add to wheat.

Chop onions fine and add to the mixture along with the remaining ingredients.

If not serving immediately, do not add tomatoes and onions until just before serving. Toss well.

Serve with Romaine lettuce leaves. Tear leaves into bite size pieces and use to scoop up salad for eating.

Serve with Kibbi Nayii (page 103), Hommous bi Tahini (page 21), Shish Kabob (page 51).

Green Bean Salad

Salatet Lubi

1 lb. green beans (fresh or frozen)	3 Tbsp. olive oil
1 clove garlic	pepper to taste
salt to taste	1 small onion (sliced in rings)
juice of 1/2 lemon	1/4 cup parsley (finely chopped)

If beans are fresh, snip ends and cut into 2 inch lengths. Cook in salted water until tender, but crisp. Drain and cool.

In salad bowl, crush garlic and salt. Add lemon juice, oil and pepper; mix well. Add green beans, onion and parsley. Toss well.

Salad may be served immediately or kept refrigerated and served at a later time for better flavor.

Saffi

1 cup chick peas (soaked overnight)	⅓ cup lemon juice
3 cups water	⅓ cup olive oil
1½ cups coarse crushed wheat	1½ tsp. salt
½ cup green onions (finely chopped)	¼ tsp. pepper
2 Tbsp. fresh mint (chopped) *or*	¼ tsp. cinnamon
1 Tbsp. dry mint	
¼ cup parsley (finely chopped)	

To remove skin from chick peas, place peas on a tea towel and roll over with a rolling pin. Place in bowl of water. Let skins float to top. Remove and drain. Place the split peas and water in saucepan. Bring to a boil over high heat, then lower heat to medium; cover and cook for 15-20 minutes until chick peas are tender (not soft). Drain and set aside.

Add enough cold water to cover crushed wheat. Set aside for 10 minutes. Drain, squeezing between hands.

Combine all ingredients in salad bowl. Toss well.

Serve with Romaine lettuce, parboiled cabbage leaves, or fresh tender grape vine leaves. Tear leaves into bite size pieces and use to scoop up salad for eating.

VARIATION:
For a hot salad, do not dispose of the liquid the chick peas were cooked in. When chick peas are tender, place with liquid in salad bowl. Add coarse burghul. Drain if necessary. Set aside for 20 minutes. Add 1 cup meat reserve (Awarma page 62) as a substitute for the oil. Combine all remaining ingredients; toss well. Serve warm with Romaine lettuce, cabbage leaves, or fresh tender grape vine leaves.

Tomato Cucumber Salad

Salatet Khiar mah Banadoora

1 medium onion (sliced in rings)	¼ cup parsley (finely chopped)
6 tomatoes (cubed)	2 Tbsp. chopped mint (optional)
2 cucumbers (sliced)	1 Lebanese Salad dressing recipe (page 42)

Place all ingredients in salad bowl. Add salad dressing and toss well.

· Serve with Meat Pies (page 135) or Stuffed Peppered Fish (page 91).

Potato Salad

Salatet Batata

6 medium potatoes
¼ cup parsley (finely chopped)
2 green onions (finely chopped)

Either one of these dressings may be used:

LEMON DRESSING
  1 clove garlic
  1 tsp. salt
  ¼ cup lemon juice
  ¼ cup olive oil

SESAME SEED DRESSING
  1 clove garlic
  1 tsp. salt
  ¼ cup Sesame Seed Paste (Tahini)
  ¼ cup lemon juice
  3 Tbsp. water

Boil potatoes with skin on. Let cool. Peel and cut into ½ inch cubes. Place in salad bowl. Add parsley and onions.

Lemon Dressing: Crush garlic with salt; add lemon juice and oil and mix well. Pour dressing over potatoes and toss gently.

Sesame Seed Dressing: Crush garlic with salt; add Sesame Seed Paste and blend well. Gradually add lemon juice, then water. Blend well. Pour over potatoes and toss gently.

Chill and serve.

Eggplant Salad

Bitinjan Mtabbel

1 large eggplant
2 green onions (with ends) chopped
1 clove garlic
1 tsp. salt (or to taste)

¼ tsp. pepper
⅓ cup lemon juice
¼ cup olive oil
parsley

Set oven at 350°F.

Pierce eggplant with fork several times, place in oven and bake for approximately 30 minutes (eggplant will be firm, but slightly soft to the touch). Run eggplant under cold water. Peel, and cut into 1 inch pieces. Place in salad bowl; add onions.

Mash garlic and salt together. Add pepper, lemon juice, olive oil and blend well. Pour dressing over eggplant and toss. May be served hot or cold. Garnish with parsley.

Serve with meatless dishes.

Cauliflower Salad

Karnabeet bi Taratour

1 medium head cauliflower	¼ cup lemon juice
1 clove garlic	¼ cup water
1 tsp. salt	1 small onion (thinly sliced)
¼ cup Sesame Seed Paste (Tahini)	¼ cup parsley (finely chopped)

Cut cauliflower into small flowerettes. Place in pot of water and parboil. Drain and leave to cool in salad bowl.

Meanwhile, in a small mixing bowl, crush garlic and salt. Add Sesame Seed Paste and blend. Gradually add lemon juice, then water, blending well. Add to cauliflower along with onions and parsley. Toss lightly.

VARIATION:
Cut cauliflower into small flowerettes but do not parboil. Use raw and prepare as above.

Spinach Salad

Salatet Sabanikh

1 large bunch spinach	¼ cup parsley (finely chopped)
1 clove garlic	3 green onions (finely chopped)
1 tsp. salt	3 Tbsp. olive oil
juice of 1 lemon	dash of pepper
2 Tbsp. fresh mint (chopped) *or*	
1 Tbsp. dry mint	

Wash spinach well. Drain and shake out excess water. Chop into bite size pieces. Set aside.

Crush garlic and salt together in a salad bowl. Add remaining ingredients and spinach. Toss well.

Serve immediately, as spinach wilts rapidly with dressing, or leave out the salt, oil and lemon juice until just before serving.

Serve with Chicken and Rice (page 81) or Salmon Steaks (page 92).

Endive Salad

Salatet Khas Murr

1 large bunch endive (approximately ½ lb.)
1 large onion (finely chopped)
¼ cup parsley (finely chopped)
½ tsp. salt (or to taste)
¼ tsp. pepper
1 clove garlic (crushed)
3 Tbsp. lemon juice
(or to taste)
3 Tbsp. olive oil

Wash endive thoroughly and chop into bite size pieces. Place in large pot of water and cook until tender but firm (approximately 15 minutes). Drain and cool.

Squeeze out excess water with both hands. Place in salad bowl and add all remaining ingredients. Toss well. Refrigerate before serving.

Serve with Fried Kafta (page 54) or Potato Fry (page 55).

VARIATION:
Wash endive; chop into bite size pieces. (Do not cook.) Proceed with method above.

Dandelion Salad

Salatet Illit

Young tender dandelion may be picked in remote fields.

1 lb. Dandelion leaves (with stems)
2 cloves garlic
1½ tsp. salt (or to taste)
¼ tsp. pepper
juice of 1 large lemon
¼ cup olive oil

Clean dandelion leaves, changing water several times. Chop into 2-3 inch pieces. Place in large pot of water with a sprinkle of salt. Bring to boil over high heat. Cover and cook over medium heat for 20-25 minutes. Drain in a colander and rinse under cold running water. Squeeze out excess water with hands. Set aside.

Crush garlic and salt together in a large salad bowl. Add cooked Dandelion, pepper, lemon juice and oil. Mix well.

To serve, tear off pieces of Pita Bread and use to scoop up salad for eating.

Serve with Potato Kibbi (page 105) or Baked Chicken and Vegetables (page 82).

VARIATION:
As an alternate dressing, use one-half a recipe of Sesame Seed Sauce (Taratour, page 26), using one whole clove of garlic.

Entrées

Lamb is plentiful in Lebanon and is a popular meat used in cooking. Lamb is the main ingredient in several entrées.

The lean meat from a leg of lamb can be used to make Kibbi, Laham Mishwi (Shish Kabob) and Kafta. The remaining meat may be chopped into cubes and used in stews or soups. It can also be ground and used in the filling for stuffed vegetables or fried with butter and added to chopped vegetables. These touches create very tasty dishes.

Because of the availability of beef in the western countries, it can be easily substituted for lamb in these recipes.

Salads, vegetables and fresh yogurt complement the foods in this section.

Top — *Shish Kabob, Rice Pilaf*
Centre — *Egg Stuffed Kafta Roll*
Bottom — *Baked Kafta*

Shish Kabob

Laham Mishwi

2 lbs. meat, beef or lamb	**salt**
2 large onions (quartered)	**pepper**
2 large peppers (cut into 1 inch cubes)	**allspice**
1 dozen cherry tomatoes	

Cut meat into 1 inch cubes and have at room temperature for 1 hour.

Alternate meat, onions, peppers and tomatoes on skewers. Sprinkle with pepper and allspice to taste. Cook over charcoal and sprinkle with salt if desired.

Serve over Rice Pilaf (page 112), or place a skewer of cooked meat and vegetables into a 7 inch Pita; wrap Pita around it and squeeze while you pull out the skewer.

Spread Chick Pea Dip (Hommous bi Tahini, page 21) or Yogurt Spread (page 124) over the cooked meat.

Note: If wooden skewers are used, soak them in water for 30 minutes before using.

VARIATION:
Meat may be marinated with ¼ cup olive oil, pepper and allspice for 1 hour before cooking.

Egg Stuffed Kafta Roll

Kafta Mahshi bi Bayd

2½-3 lbs. ground lean beef or lamb	**2 tsp. salt**
1 medium onion (grated)	**¼ tsp. pepper**
¼ tsp. cinnamon	**1 cup parsley (finely chopped)**
¼ tsp. allspice	**6 eggs (hard boiled and peeled)**

Set oven at 350°F.

Combine and thoroughly mix first six ingredients. Divide meat into two sections, flattening each into approximately ¾ inch thickness, keeping the meat in a rectangle shape. Sprinkle half of the parsley across the top of each. Place 3 eggs across the length of the rectangle over the parsley and roll (as in jelly roll). Wet hands and smooth the outside well, sealing the edges all over. Place in buttered pan side by side.

Bake for approximately 1 hour, or until meat is cooked through.

To serve, cut into 1 inch thick slices. Serve with salads, or Chick Pea Dip (Hommous bi Tahini, page 21).

Baked Kafta
Kafta bi Saneah

1 lb. ground beef or lamb	2 medium potatoes (sliced)
1 medium onion (grated)	2 medium carrots (sliced)
1 tsp. salt	1/2 tsp. salt
1/4 tsp. pepper	1/4 tsp. pepper
1/4 cup parsley (finely chopped)	1/2 tsp. cinnamon
1/4 cup vegetable oil (for frying)	1/4 cup tomato paste
2 zucchini, 6-8 inches long (sliced)	3 cups water

Set oven at 375°F. Combine meat, onion, 1 teaspoon salt, 1/4 teaspoon pepper and parsley. Mix well.

Form into 1 1/2 inch balls then flatten into patties and fry slightly in a skillet with the oil, turning over once, (do not cook through). Remove from skillet and place in a baking or casserole dish.

Combine remaining ingredients and add to meat patties. Stir gently. Bake for 45-60 minutes or until carrots are tender.

Serve with Rice Pilaf (page 112).

Barbequed Kafta
Kafta Mishwi

1 1/2 lbs. ground lean beef or lamb	1/4 tsp. cayenne
1 medium onion (grated)	1/4 tsp. allspice
1/2 cup parsley (finely chopped)	1/4 tsp. pepper
1 1/2 tsp. salt	

Metal or wooden skewers may be used. Combine and mix all ingredients well. Take a small amount from the mixture and wrap around the length of the skewer, pressing firmly. Cook over charcoal. Do not overcook.

Serve with Hommous bi Tahini (page 21), Yogurt Cucumber Salad (page 122), Tabouli (page 43), or inside Pita Bread pockets.

VARIATION:

(1) To broil in oven, form into small rolls resembling fingers. Cook on cookie sheet under broiler. Turn over to cook the other side. May be placed on barbeque grill instead of a skewer.

(2) Form into small balls and place on cookie sheet. Cook under broiler.

Kafta-Potato Bake

Kafta mah Batata

2 lbs. ground lean beef or lamb
1 medium onion (finely chopped)
½ cup parsley (finely chopped)
2 tsp. salt
¼ tsp. pepper
¼ tsp. allspice

4 medium potatoes
¼ cup tomato paste
2 cups water
dash salt
dash cinnamon

Set oven at 350°F. Thoroughly mix first 6 ingredients. Spread mixture into a greased 9x12 inch baking pan.

Peel potatoes and slice into ½ inch thick slices and place evenly on top of meat layer.

Blend the tomato paste with the water and pour over the potato layer. Sprinkle a dash of salt and cinnamon over potatoes. Bake for 45-60 minutes, or until meat is cooked.

Serve with Rice Pilaf (page 112).

Grilled Kafta

Kafta bi Kmaj

1 lb. ground lean beef or lamb
1 medium onion (grated)
½ cup parsley (finely chopped)
½ tsp. allspice

1 tsp. salt
¼ tsp. pepper
4 7" Pita Bread
¼ cup butter (for frying)

Combine all ingredients, except Pita Bread and butter, in a mixing bowl. Mix well. Split Pita around the edges of the round, leaving approximately 3 inches attached. Divide the mixture among the 4 Pita and spread meat inside. Fold the top layer of the Pita over the meat.

Place heavy skillet over low to medium heat and add a ½ teaspoon of the butter. Grill the meat filled Pita, pressing down a few times until golden brown. Add another ½ teaspoon of butter. Flip over and grill the other side. Place the Pita as you cook it in a 200°F oven to keep warm.

May be served with pickles and raw vegetables for lunch.

VARIATION:
(1) After meat is spread in the Pita, bake in oven at 350°F for 10-15 minutes or until meat is cooked.
(2) Spread meat inside Pita and grill on barbeque over charcoal.

Fried Kafta

Kafta Makli

1 ½ lbs. lean ground beef or lamb
  1 small onion (grated)
  ¼ cup parsley (finely chopped)
1 ½ tsp. salt

¼ tsp. pepper
¼ tsp. cumin
¼ cup vegetable oil
  (for frying)

Combine all ingredients except vegetable oil in a mixing bowl. Form into balls the size of an egg. Flatten to form a pattie.

Heat oil in skillet for frying. Fry each pattie, turning once.

Serve with fresh vegetables or pickles inside Pita Bread pockets.

Leg of Lamb

1 leg of lamb (4 - 5 lbs.)
2 tsp. salt
½ tsp. pepper
½ tsp. allspice

6-8 garlic cloves
¼ cup parsley (finely chopped)
1 cup water

Set oven at 325 °F. Allow 30 minutes cooking time for every pound of lamb. Rub seasonings all over the meat.

Insert a knife into 6 - 8 different spots of the leg of lamb. Stuff a garlic clove and a teaspoon of parsley into each incision.

Place water in roasting pan. Put the leg of lamb on the rack of the roasting pan and cover. Baste occasionally until meat is cooked.

Serve sliced lamb pieces over Rice Pilaf (page 112).

Potato Fry

M'farakit Batata

4 cups potatoes (diced small)
1 tsp. salt
¾ cup ground beef *or* meat reserve
(Awarma - page 62)

1 medium onion (coarsely chopped)
1¼ tsp. salt (or to taste)
¼ tsp. pepper

Place diced potatoes in cold water and 1 teaspoon salt and set aside.

Place meat and onion in skillet. Sauté until onion is transparent.

Add drained potatoes, salt and pepper. Cook (uncovered) over medium heat until potatoes are tender, stirring occasionally to prevent sticking.

Serve with fresh plain yogurt, pickles, and fresh vegetables.

VARIATION:
(1) Substitute diced zucchini for potatoes.
(2) After potatoes (or zucchini) are tender, break 4 eggs over the mixture, stirring gently to break the yolk. Cook slightly until eggs are set.

Eggs with Tomatoes

Bayd mah Banadoora

6 medium, ripe tomatoes
½ cup ground beef *or* meat reserve
(Awarma - page 62)
1 medium onion (diced)

1 tsp. salt (or to taste)
¼ tsp. pepper
4 eggs

Add boiling water to tomatoes, remove skin and dice. Set aside.

Place meat in skillet, add onions and sauté over medium heat until onions are transparent. Add tomatoes, salt and pepper. Turn heat to low, and cook until tomatoes are soft and some of the liquid from the tomatoes has evaporated (approximately 30 minutes).

Drop in eggs, breaking the yolk. Stir occasionally until eggs are slightly cooked.

Serve hot or cold for lunch. May be served with Fried Cauliflower (page 115), olives, yogurt.

VARIATION:
Omit meat and sauté onion in 2 tablespoons butter following same directions.

Lamb-Vegetable Casserole

Laham mah Khodra

1 lb. lamb shoulder (cut into very small cubes)	2 zucchini
3 Tbsp. butter	1 large onion
2 large potatoes	2 tsp. salt (or to taste)
1 large eggplant	¼ tsp. pepper
4 large ripe tomatoes	¼ tsp. cinnamon
	water

Place meat in skillet with the butter and sauté until meat is slightly browned. Set aside.

Set oven at 375 °F. Peel potatoes and eggplant and cut into ½ inch thick slices. Cut tomatoes and zucchini into ½ inch thick slices (do not peel). Slice onions into thin rings.

Layer ingredients in a 9x12 inch baking pan. Begin with the potatoes, then the zucchini, meat, eggplant, tomatoes and the onions on top. Add enough water to barely cover the vegetables. Sprinkle seasonings over top. Cover and bake for 50-60 minutes.

Serve with Rice Pilaf (page 112).

Meatballs in Tahini Sauce

Kafta bi Taratour

1½ lbs. ground lean beef or lamb	¼ tsp. pepper
1 small onion (minced)	¼ cup parsley (finely chopped)
3 cloves garlic (crushed)	1 recipe Sesame Seed Sauce (page 26)
1½ tsp. salt.	(add ½ cup water to this recipe)

Heat oven at 400 °F. Mix together all above ingredients except recipe for Sesame Seed Sauce. Form into small balls the size of marbles. Place in a baking dish and bake for 15-20 minutes or until meat is cooked.

Meanwhile, prepare Sesame Seed Sauce. Pour over cooked meat balls. Return to oven and bake until sauce bubbles.

Serve hot as sauce will thicken as it cools. Lemon juice may be squeezed over individual servings.

Meatballs in Tomato Sauce

1½ lbs. lean ground beef or lamb
1 small onion (grated)
¼ tsp. allspice
1 tsp. salt
¼ tsp. pepper
1 cup pine nuts
½ cup vegetable oil

2 large onions (coarsely chopped)
5 ripe medium tomatoes (peeled)
2 Tbsp. tomato paste
1½ cups water
½ tsp. allspice
salt and pepper to taste
juice of ½ lemon

Place ground meat, grated onions, ¼ teaspoon allspice, 1 teaspoon salt and ¼ teaspoon pepper in a mixing bowl. Mix well. Form into walnut size balls. Set aside.

In a saucepan lightly brown the pine nuts in the oil. Remove pine nuts from oil onto a small plate. Leave aside. Place chopped onions in the same oil and fry until golden brown. Remove onions from oil and place on another small plate. Set aside.

Place the tomatoes, tomato paste and water in the same saucepan and bring to boil on high heat. Add remaining seasonings and lemon juice. Add meatballs and browned onions. Simmer for 25-30 minutes. Add the pine nuts just before serving.

Serve with meatballs over Rice Pilaf (page 112).

Stews

The popularity of stews has existed for centuries throughout the Middle East. Even today, stews top the list of foods when the Lebanese home-maker is at a loss for a dish to cook for lunch or dinner.

Tomato paste, vegetables, chick peas and legumes are essential for most Lebanese stews. These healthy ingredients result in a delicious and hearty meal that is both simple and economical.

Meat Reserve (Awarma) may be successfully substituted for meat in any of the recipes in this section. And for the vegetarian, meat can be easily omitted and replaced with ¼ cup vegetable oil, or as specified in the recipes in this book. The result is a meatless stew, delicious hot or cold.

Stew dishes, which may be seasoned to meet the individual palate, are usually accompanied by Rice Pilaf and Pita bread pieces.

Green Bean Meat Stew

Green Bean Meat Stew

Lubi bi Laham

1 lb. beef or lamb (cut into ½ inch cubes)
3 Tbsp. butter or vegetable oil
1 medium onion (finely chopped)
2 lbs. green beans (fresh or frozen)
   water

¼ cup tomato paste
1½ tsp. salt
¼ tsp. pepper
¼ tsp. cinnamon

If beans are fresh, snip ends and cut into 2 inch lengths. Wash and drain. If frozen, use as is.

In saucepan, sauté meat in oil or butter until meat is browned. Add chopped onion. Sauté until onion is limp. Add beans, stir, then add water to cover. Cover and cook until meat and beans are tender, 40-50 minutes.

Add tomato paste, salt, pepper and cinnamon. Cook an additional 10-15 minutes.

Serve with Rice Pilaf (page 112), Kibbi Balls (page 101), hot pickles.

Green Bean Stew

Lubi bi Ziet

Meatless

½ cup chick peas (soaked overnight)
2 lbs. green beans (fresh or frozen)
1 medium onion (diced)
¼ cup vegetable oil
1 clove garlic (crushed)

1½ tsp. salt
¼ tsp. pepper
½ tsp. cinnamon
   water
¼ cup tomato paste

Drain chick peas, place on tea towel, roll over with rolling pin to crack the peas. Discard skin.

If beans are fresh, snip ends and cut into 2 inch lengths. Wash and drain. If frozen, use as is.

In saucepan, sauté onions and garlic in oil until light brown. Add beans, chick peas and seasonings to onion mixture and toss lightly. Cover and simmer for 5 minutes.

Add water to cover beans and cook for 30 minutes on medium heat. Add tomato paste. Stir slightly, cover and cook for another 15-20 minutes, until beans are tender.

Serve with Rice Pilaf (page 112) or Potato Omelet (page 111).

Zucchini-Potato Stew

Yakhnit Koosa mah Batata

½ lb. beef or lamb (ground)
3 Tbsp. vegetable oil
1 medium onion (diced)
3 zucchini 6 inches long
   (sliced into ½ inch slices)
4 large potatoes (in 1 inch cubes)

1 tsp. salt (or to taste)
¼ tsp. pepper
¼ tsp. cinnamon
4 Tbsp. tomato paste
   water

Brown meat in oil and add onion. Sauté until onion is limp. Add zucchini and potatoes. Stir for 1 minute.

Add seasonings, tomato paste and enough water to just cover the mixture. Cover and cook over medium heat until vegetables are tender, approximately 30 minutes.

Serve with Stuffed Chicken (page 83), Lebanese Salad (page 41) and Rice Pilaf (page 112).

VARIATION:
To make Potato Stew: Use 7 large potatoes and omit zucchini.

Meat Reserve

Awarma

This meat reserve was used in the Middle East where there was no refrigeration or easy access to fresh meat. It keeps well in a cool, dry place. Awarma is used in Lebanese homes to this day.

2 lbs. beef fat (ground)
3 lbs. lean beef or lamb (ground coarse)

2 Tbsp. salt

Cook the fat over medium heat in saucepan, boiling approximately 25 minutes until the fat has melted and shrunk. Drain through a sieve into another saucepan. Discard the suet, and save the liquid.

Add the meat to liquid from the drained fat. Add salt, stir and cook until the meat changes color. Bring to boil over medium-high heat then turn to medium-low heat and cook for about 30-40 minutes, stirring occasionally.

Meat is ready when you take a large spoon of the mixture and liquid, and it is still bubbling in the spoon. Cool, then pour in casserole dish or appropriate container. Cover and store in refrigerator. Keeps well for 1-2 months.

Uses: In stew dishes replacing cubed or ground meat, using the same amount of Awarma to replace fresh meat. In place of ground meat for vegetable stuffings. Warm a few tablespoons in a frying pan, add eggs and scramble.

Eggplant and Lamb Stew

Bitinjan mah Laham

1 lb. lamb shoulder (cut into ½" cubes)	¼ cup vegetable oil
3 Tbsp. flour	1 large onion (finely chopped)
1½ tsp. salt	2 cloves garlic (crushed)
½ tsp. pepper	2 cups tomato sauce
½ tsp. cinnamon	½ cup water
	1 large eggplant

Coat meat with the mixture of flour, salt, pepper and cinnamon. Place oil in saucepan, add meat and brown over medium heat. Add onion and garlic and sauté until onions are limp. Add tomato sauce and water. Cover and cook on low heat for 45-50 minutes or until meat is tender.

Peel eggplant, cut into 1 inch cubes and add to meat mixture. Cook for 30 minutes.

Service with Rice Pilaf (page 112).

Macaroni in Tomato Sauce

Ma'karuni bi Banadoora

½ lb. lean beef or lamb (ground)	1½ tsp. salt (or to taste)
3 Tbsp. vegetable oil	¼ tsp. pepper
1 medium onion (finely chopped)	½ tsp. cinnamon
1 clove garlic (crushed)	3 cups water
¼ cup tomato paste	2 cups elbow macaroni

Place meat in saucepan with the oil. Sauté until meat is browned. Add onions and garlic and sauté until onions are transparent. Add tomato paste, seasonings and water and cook over medium heat for 15 minutes.

While sauce is cooking, place the macaroni in a pot of boiling water with a dash of salt and cook until tender (approximately 10-15 minutes). Drain and add to the cooking sauce. Cook for another 5 minutes.

Serve with Rice Pilaf (page 112).

Bean Stew

Fasoolia

½ lb. beef or lamb (cut into ½" cubes)	water
3 Tbsp. vegetable oil	1½ tsp. salt
1 clove garlic (crushed)	¼ tsp. pepper
1 medium onion (diced)	½ tsp. cinnamon
1 lb. kidney, lima or navy beans (soaked overnight)	¼ cup tomato paste

Sauté meat with oil in saucepan until meat is brown. Add garlic and onions and continue to sauté until onions are limp. Drain beans and add to mixture. Stir for 1 minute over heat. Add water even with bean level. Add salt, pepper and cinnamon. Bring to a boil, cover and cook over medium heat until beans are tender, stirring occasionally.

Add tomato paste. Simmer for 10 minutes.

Serve with Rice Pilaf (page 112).

Upside Down Eggplant Casserole

Ma'aloobi

½ cup pine nuts	4 large tomatoes
2 Tbsp. butter or vegetable oil	1 large onion
1½ lbs. lean beef or lamb (ground)	1 tsp. salt
1 medium onion (finely chopped)	½ tsp. pepper
1½ tsp. salt	½ tsp. cinnamon
¼ tsp. pepper	½ cup tomato paste
2 large eggplants	2½ cups water
4 large potatoes	

Sauté pine nuts and butter in skillet until nuts are golden brown. Add meat and chopped onion. Sauté until meat changes color. Add 1½ teaspoons salt and ¼ teaspoon pepper. Set aside.

Heat oven to 350°F. Peel eggplant and potatoes. Cut both into ½ inch thick slices. Cut tomatoes and onions into ¼ inch thick slices. Divide the vegetables evenly into two groups.

Layer the first group by alternating the four vegetables in a casserole dish. Spread the meat filling evenly over the vegetables. Layer the remaining vegetables over the filling. Add the salt, pepper and cinnamon. Mix the tomato paste and water together in a small bowl and pour on top. Cover with lid and bake for 1 hour or until all vegetables are tender.

Serve with Rice Pilaf (page 112).

Lima Bean and Lamb Stew

Fasoolia mah Laham

1 lb. lamb shoulder (cubed into ½" pieces)	4 large ripe tomatoes
3 Tbsp. vegetable oil	2 lbs. lima beans (frozen)
1 medium onion (finely chopped)	1½ tsp. salt (or to taste)
2 cloves garlic (crushed)	¼ tsp. pepper
water	½ tsp. cinnamon

Place the meat in a saucepan with the oil. Sauté over medium heat until meat changes color. Add onions and garlic and sauté until onions are transparent. Add enough water to cover the meat, then add the tomatoes. Bring to a boil over high heat.

Lower heat to medium, cover and cook until meat is tender (approximately 30-40 minutes).

Add frozen lima beans and seasonings to meat mixture. Add enough water to barely cover mixture. Bring to boil again. Turn heat to low, cover and cook for 25-30 minutes or until beans are tender.

Serve with Rice Pilaf (page 112).

Lamb Stew

Laham bi Khodra

2 lbs. lamb shoulder (cut into 1" cubes)	1 5½ oz. can tomato paste
3 Tbsp. vegetable oil	1½ tsp. salt
1 large onion (quartered)	½ tsp. pepper
2 cloves garlic (crushed)	½ tsp. cinnamon
2 zucchini (6" long - sliced thick)	½ tsp. basil
2 large carrots (sliced thin)	water
1 lb. fresh mushrooms (whole)	

In a small roasting pan place meat, oil, onion and garlic. Stir-fry over medium heat until meat is brown. Add water to cover. Bring to a boil. Cover with lid. Place in 450°F oven and cook for 45 minutes, or until meat is tender.

Add remaining ingredients and additional water to cover the mixture. Return to oven and continue cooking until vegetables are tender (approximately 20-25 minutes).

Serve with Rice Pilaf (page 112), Kibbi bi Saneah (page 102), and raw vegetables.

Lentil-Vegetable Stew
Adas mah Khodra

10 cups water
2 cups lentils
2 lbs. beef ribs
1 cup green beans
3 large tomatoes (diced)
1 cup cabbage (diced)

3 carrots (sliced)
2 zucchini (sliced 1 inch thick)
1½ tsp. salt
½ tsp. pepper
1 tsp. fine herbs (sold in spice department)

Combine water, lentils and ribs in large skillet. Bring to boil over high heat, then lower heat to medium. Skim off foam. Cover and cook until lentils are tender, approximately 1 hour.

Trim green beans and cut into 1 inch pieces. Add to lentil mixture along with remaining ingredients. Cook until vegetables are tender (approximately 30 minutes).

Serve with Fried Cauliflower (page 115).

Spinach Stew
Sabanikh mah Laham

1 lb. beef or lamb (cubed into ½" pieces)
1 small onion (whole)
   water
1 lb. fresh spinach
4 Tbsp. butter
1 small onion (diced small)

1 clove garlic (crushed)
1½ tsp. salt
½ tsp. pepper
¼ tsp. coriander powder
   juice of ½ lemon

Place meat and the whole onion in a large saucepan. Add enough water to cover. Bring to a boil over high heat.

Skim off foam. Cover and cook over medium-low heat until meat is tender (approximately 50-60 minutes).

Wash spinach well and chop into large pieces, set aside. Melt butter in a large saucepan. Add diced onion and garlic. Sauté until onions are limp. Add spinach and seasonings. Cook over medium heat until spinach has wilted, occasionally turning over the spinach with a wooden spoon.

Add meat and broth to spinach mixture. Cover and cook for 10-15 minutes over low heat.

Squeeze lemon juice over top of spinach mixture.

Serve with Rice Pilaf (page 112).

Artichoke and Lamb Stew

Ardishowki mah Laham

8 fresh artichokes	3 cups water
1/3 cup lemon juice	1 1/2 tsp. salt
1/3 cup vegetable oil	1/2 tsp. pepper
1 lb. beef or lamb (cubed small)	1/3 cup lemon juice
1 large onion (coarsely chopped)	1/4 cup parsley

Wash artichokes well. Cut off stems and break off the tough outside leaves. Remove fuzzy choke from inside. Cut artichoke into fourths, lengthwise, and place them in a bowl and add lemon juice. Toss well and set aside fro 10-15 minutes.

Drain artichokes well (save the lemon juice).

Heat oil for frying. Fry artichokes until slightly golden (frying will retain the shape of the artichoke in the stew). Remove from oil onto a plate. Set aside.

Fry the meat cubes in the same oil until browned. Add onions and saute until transparent. Add water. Place all the meat mixture into a saucepan adding salt and pepper. Bring to boil. Turn heat to low, cover and simmer for 45 minutes.

Add artichokes and save lemon juice, adding a little more water to cover. Adjust seasoning to taste. Cover and simmer for another 30 minutes. Then remove the cover, and simmer for 10-15 minutes, so some of the water evaporates. Sprinkle parsley on top.

Serve with Rice Pilaf (page 112).

Stuffed Vegetables
(Mahshi)

Unique dishes can be created by using vegetable leaves such as grape vine leaves, cabbage, Swiss Chard and spinach, to wrap rice and meat fillings. (Vegetarians may prefer a lenten filling). These dishes are easy to make, although they are a little time consuming. The flavourful result is delicious, hot or cold. A sandwich-like dish can be created by placing the stuffed leaves in a Pita Bread and rolling.

Another succulent creation involves hollowing out vegetables (whether zucchini, eggplant, tomatoes, peppers or potatoes) and stuffing them with a delicious rice and meat filling.

Spices and herbs are extremely important additions to most Middle Eastern foods. Used cautiously, they create an unusual and delicate flavour.

Stuffed vegetables are often served with fresh yogurt.

Top — *Stuffed Zucchini*
Bottom — *Stuffed Tomatoes*

Stuffed Zucchini

Koosa Mahshi

8 zucchini *or* vegetable marrow (5 -6" long)	¼ tsp. pepper
¾ cup rice (washed and drained)	½ tsp. cinnamon
1 cup beef or lamb (ground)	2 Tbsp. butter
1½ tsp. salt	1 5½ oz. can tomato paste
	water

Cut off the growth end of zucchini or vegetable marrow. Hollow vegetables out by using a table knife, apple corer or a special zucchini corer, removing the pulp and leaving a ¼ inch wall. Be careful not to pierce walls. Set aside.

Set oven at 400°F.

Mix all other ingredients together except tomato paste and water. Stuff the zucchini or vegetable marrow with the mixture to within ½ inch from the top. Lay side by side in a small roasting pan. Mix the tomato paste with 1 cup water and pour over the stuffed vegetables. Then, add enough water to cover the vegetables. Cover and bake for 60 minutes or until rice is cooked.

Serve with fresh Yogurt (page 123) or Lebanese Salad (page 41).

Note: Use the pulp of zucchini to make Zucchini Omelet (page 113).

Cabbage Rolls

Malfoof

1 cabbage (medium head)	½ tsp. pepper
1 cup rice (washed and drained)	½ tsp. cinnamon
1 cup beef or lamb (ground)	2 Tbsp. lemon juice
3 Tbsp. butter	1 5½ oz. can of tomato paste
1 clove garlic (crushed)	water
2 tsp. salt	

Core and parboil cabbage until limp. Cut leaves in half, removing the ribs.

Set oven at 400°F.

Combine all ingredients except cabbage leaves, tomato paste and water. Place a heaping tablespoon of the filling in a leaf lengthwise. Fold the outside edges ½ inch towards centre and roll. Arrange in a casserole dish or small roaster. Mix the tomato paste with 1 cup of water and pour over the rolls. Then, add additional water to just above the level of the rolls. Cover and bake for 60 minutes or until rice is tender.

Serve with Tomato Cucumber Salad (page 44) or fresh yogurt.

Stuffed Tomatoes

Banadoora Mahshi

6 large tomatoes	1 ½ tsp. salt
½ cup pine nuts	¼ tsp. pepper
3 Tbsp. butter	¼ tsp. cinnamon
1 lb. beef or lamb (ground)	2 cups crushed tomatoes
1 medium onion (finely chopped)	(canned or fresh)
	1 cup water

Set oven at 400°F. Make a 1 inch opening in the stem end of the tomato. Hollow out the pulp (save the pulp to add to filling).

In a frying pan, sauté the pine nuts in the butter until golden brown. Add meat and onions and sauté until meat changes color but do not fully cook. Add salt, pepper, cinnamon and tomato pulp. Remove from heat. Stuff hollowed tomatoes with meat mixture to within ¼ inch of top. Arrange upright in a baking dish. Pour the crushed tomatoes over top. Add water to bottom of baking dish. Cover and bake for 40-50 minutes or until done.

Serve with salads.

VARIATION:
Potatoes or green peppers may be used instead of tomatoes. If using potatoes, peel and core, leaving a ½ inch wall. If using peppers, remove stem and hollow out seeds, following the same method as above.

Lenten Stuffing

Hashwi Bedoun Laham   Meatless

½ cup chick peas (soaked overnight)	2 medium tomatoes (finely diced)
1 ½ cups rice (washed and drained)	1 ½ tsp. salt
½ cup parsley (finely chopped)	¼ tsp. pepper
½ cup green onions (finely chopped)	¼ tsp. cinnamon
2 Tbsp. fresh mint (chopped) *or*	¾ cup vegetable oil
1 Tbsp. dry	½ cup lemon juice

Drain chick peas and place on tea towel. Roll over with a rolling pin to crack the skin. Place in a mixing bowl with 3 - 4 cups water. Remove the skin that floats to the top and discard. Drain. Add all remaining ingredients. Mix well. This recipe may be used for filling any vegetables, grape vine leaves and Swiss Chard leaves.

Stuffed Grapevine Leaves

Warak Dawali

Grapevine leaves, preserved in jars, may be found in specialty foodstores.

40-50 grapevine leaves
1 cup rice (washed and drained)
½ lb. beef or lamb (ground)
1½ tsp. salt
¼ tsp. pepper

¼ tsp. cinnamon
2 Tbsp. butter
juice of one lemon
water

If using preserved grape leaves, soak in cold water for 1 hour, replacing water several times to remove salt. If using fresh leaves, let stand in hot water for 10 minutes to soften.

Combine all ingredients except grape leaves, lemon and water in mixing bowl. Place 1 teaspoon (or more, depending on size of leaf) of the meat mixture in a thin row across the width of the leaf with the stemmed end closest to you and the shiny side of the leaf facing down. Fold the outside edges of the leaf ½ inch toward the centre and roll with a little firmness into the shape of a finger. Place in saucepan, alternating the direction of each layer.

When all leaves are rolled, sprinkle with lemon juice. Add enough water to just below top level of rolls. Bring to a boil, then lower heat, cover and simmer for 45 minutes until leaves are tender.

Serve with cold, fresh Yogurt (page 123), Tabouli (page 43).

VARIATION:
(1) Two large tomatoes (skinned and chopped), or stewed canned tomatoes may be added to the filling.
(2) Lenten Stuffing (page 72) may be substituted for above meat filling.
(3) Fresh rhubarb stalks may be spread over top of the rolls instead of lemon juice.

Stuffed Swiss Chard

Silque Mahshi   Meatless

40-50 **Swiss Chard leaves**
  1 **cup rice (washed and drained)**
  ½ **cup dry chick peas**
    (soaked overnight)
  ½ **cup vegetable oil**
1½ **tsp. salt**
  ¼ **tsp. pepper**

6 **green onions (finely chopped)**
1 **cup lemon juice**
2 **Tbsp. dry mint** *or*
4 **Tbsp. fresh mint (chopped)**
¾ **cup parsley (finely chopped)**
  water

Using fresh Swiss Chard, place leaves in hot water for 10 minutes to soften for rolling (if the leaves are too large cut in half). Remove the ribs from the leaf. Set leaves aside.

Drain chick peas and place on tea towel. Roll over with rolling pin to crack the skin and remove the skin from the peas or place the peas in a bowl of water so the skin will float to surface.

Combine the skinned chick peas, *half* of the lemon juice, and all other ingredients except Swiss Chard and water. Mix well.

Place a tablespoon of the filling lengthwise on a leaf bringing the edges about ½ inch toward the centre and rolling as fingers. Arrange in saucepan, alternating the direction of each layer. Add the other ½ cup lemon juice and enough water to reach just below the level of the last row. Bring to boil, then cover and simmer for 45 - 60 minutes. All water should have evaporated. If not, remove lid and simmer for a further 10 minutes.

Place a plate over top of the pan and holding plate and pot securely together, turn upsidedown so all the rolls remain in the same mold on the plate as the pan.

Serve with yogurt, Kibbi Balls (page 101), Fried Cauliflower (page 115).

VARIATION:
Two large tomatoes (skinned and chopped) or stewed canned tomatoes may be added to the filling.

Lamb Stuffed Zucchini

Ablama

½ lb. lamb shoulder	1 medium onion (finely chopped)
(coarsely ground)	8 small zucchini
¼ tsp. cinnamon	(5 - 6" in length)
1 tsp. salt	¼ cup butter or margarine
¼ tsp. pepper	2 cups tomato sauce
½ cup pine nuts	water

Sauté meat with seasonings and pine nuts until lightly browned. Add onions and sauté until onions are transparent. Set aside.

Set oven at 400°F.

Trim both ends of the zucchini and rinse. Lightly brown with the butter in a skillet over low to medium heat until zucchini is soft. Remove with a lifter onto a platter. Make a slit lengthwise into the zucchini. Stuff with 2 tablespoons of the filling. Arrange side by side in a baking dish, the slit side up. Pour tomato sauce over top and add enough water to cover. Sprinkle a dash of salt over top.

Bake in oven for 40-50 minutes.

Serve with Rice Pilaf (page 112).

Stuffed Spinach Leaves

Sabanikh Mahshi   Meatless

2 lbs. spinach (only the leaves)	¼ cup lemon juice
1 recipe Lenten Stuffing (page 72)	½ tsp. salt
2 cloves garlic (crushed)	water

Place spinach leaves in hot water for 10 minutes to soften.

Place 2 tablespoons of the stuffing across the width of the leaf, bringing the two outside edges about 1 inch toward the centre and rolling into a finger shape. Place in a saucepan side by side and snugly against each other. Layer until all have been rolled.

Mix garlic, lemon juice and salt together and pour over the rolls.

Place a small, heat proof plate upside down inside the pan over the rolls. Press down on the plate and while pressing add enough water to cover the plate.

Bring to a boil, cover and simmer for 45-50 minutes.

Serve with fresh yogurt or salads.

Stuffed Eggplant
Sheik el Mahshi

Very small eggplant may be found in specialty food stores in season.

½ cup pine nuts
2 Tbsp. butter
½ lb. beef or lamb (ground)
¼ tsp. pepper
½ tsp. cinnamon
1 tsp. salt
1 medium onion (chopped)

1 tomato (finely diced)
6 eggplants (4 - 5″ long, or 3 large)
3 Tbsp. butter
2 cups tomato sauce
   water
2 Tbsp. dry mint

Set oven at 350°F.

Sauté pine nuts with 2 tablespoons butter until golden brown. Add meat, salt, pepper and cinnamon and stir well. Add onion and sauté until onions are limp and meat is browned. Add the diced tomato and set aside.

Peel eggplants, cutting off the stems. Place in frying pan with the 3 tablespoons butter, browning all sides until barely soft. Remove and place on platter. Make a lengthwise slit in each eggplant, reaching only to the centre. Stuff with filling.

Arrange in baking dish side by side, slit side up. Pour tomato sauce over the eggplant, adding water to just below top of eggplant level.

Sprinkle dry mint over top. Cover and bake for 50-60 minutes. Remove gently onto platter with a lifter. If using large eggplant, cut into serving pieces after removing from oven.

Serve with Rice Pilaf (page 112), Hommous bi Tahini (page 21).

VARIATION:
Substitute potatoes for eggplants. Core and fry, then fill, following method above.

Burghul Stuffing

Hashwi bi Burghul Meatless

½ cup chick peas (soaked overnight)
2 cups coarse crushed wheat
¼ cup parsley (finely chopped)
¼ cup green onions (finely chopped)
1 Tbsp. fresh mint (chopped) *or*
1 tsp. dry

2 tsp. salt
¼ tsp pepper
¼ tsp. cinnamon
¼ cup vegetable oil

Drain chick peas and place them on a tea towel. Roll over with a rolling pin to crack the skin. Place in a mixing bowl with 3-4 cups of water. Remove the skin that floats to the top and discard. Drain and add all remaining ingredients. Mix well.

This stuffing is excellent for stuffing grape vine leaves, swiss chard, spinach or cabbage. All other hollowed out vegetables may also be stuffed following the directions for cooking the individual recipes in this section. A little more or less chick peas may be used or omit the chick peas altogether.

This meatless stuffing is excellent served hot or cold, with fresh cold yogurt or salads.

VARIATION:
⅓ cup meat reserve (Awarma page 62) may be substituted for the oil following the same directions. Serve this hot.

Poultry

Chicken, whether stuffed, barbequed or cut up and cooked with vegetables, is always a pleasure to serve. Many chicken dishes are easy to make; they can be prepared ahead and kept in the refrigerator until cooking time.

In Lebanon chicken is plentiful and with added ingredients, spices and herbs, the flavor is unforgettable. Two favorites included in this section are Lemon Chicken, which is marinated in lemon juice, and Chicken with Bread, which is prepared with a typical Lebanese spice – sumac. These two tangy flavors compliment the chicken very nicely.

Top — *Chicken and Rice*
Bottom — *Baked Chicken and Vegetables*

Chicken and Rice

Djaj mah Ruz

Step (a)
 1 roasting chicken (whole)
 1 tsp. salt
 ½ tsp. pepper

 ¼ tsp. cinnamon
 2 Tbsp. butter
 1 clove garlic (crushed)

Step (b) Stuffing
 ¼ cup butter
 1 cup beef or lamb (ground)
 1 cup long grain rice
 1 tsp. salt (or to taste)

 ¼ tsp. pepper
 ¼ tsp. cinnamon
 1½ cups water

Step (c)
 ¼ cup slivered almonds
 ¼ cup pine nuts

 ¼ cup unsalted butter
 ½ cup seedless raisins (optional)

Set oven at 450°F.

(a) Clean chicken and rub all over with remaining ingredients. Place in roasting pan with ½ cup water. Bake for 1¼ hours or until chicken is tender.

(b) While chicken is cooking prepare stuffing on top of stove. In saucepan sauté butter and meat until meat is brown. Add the washed and drained rice, salt, pepper and cinnamon. Sauté for 1 minute, add water. Bring to boil over high heat. Lower heat, cover and simmer for 30 minutes, or until rice is tender.

(c) While rice is cooking, sauté nuts in butter until golden brown. Add raisins and sauté for 1 minute.

To serve, debone chicken. Set aside. Place rice stuffing on large platter. Arrange chicken pieces over top of rice and sprinkle nuts and raisins over the chicken.

Serve with Kibbi Nayii (page 103), Bean Salad (page 41), or Eggplant-Chick Pea Stew (page 116).

Baked Chicken and Vegetables

Djaj mah Khodra

1 frying chicken (cut up)
¼ cup vegetable oil
2 green peppers (sliced into rounds)
2 large tomatoes (sliced into rounds)
1 large onion (sliced into rounds)
2 6″ zucchini (sliced into rounds)

2 medium potatoes (peeled, sliced into rounds)
1½ tsp. salt
½ tsp. pepper
1 tsp. basil
2 cloves garlic (crushed)
2 Tbsp. parsley (chopped)

Set oven at 400°F. Wash and dry chicken. Place in a baking pan. Add oil then all remaining ingredients. Mix well, coating the chicken and vegetables with the oil. Bake for 1 hour or until chicken is tender.

Serve with Rice Pilaf (page 112), Potato Omelet (page 111), or Lebanese Salad (page 41).

Chicken Rice Pilaf

Djaj mah Ruz M'falfal

½ chicken
5 cups water
½ cup almonds (blanched)
¼ cup pine nuts
3 Tbsp. butter

2 cups rice (soaked for 30 minutes)
3 cups chicken broth
1½ tsp. salt
¼ tsp. pepper
cinnamon

Cook chicken in the water until tender. Remove from liquid, debone and set aside. Save the liquid.

Place almonds, pine nuts and butter in a saucepan. Turn heat to low. Stir browning the nuts to a golden color. Drain rice and add to the nuts. Stir on low heat for 1 minute. Add chicken pieces, broth, salt and pepper. Bring to boil on high heat, lower heat, cover and simmer for 20-25 minutes.

Serve on a platter with a sprinkle of cinnamon over top.

Stuffed Chicken

Djaj Mahshi

¾ cup rice	¼ tsp. cinnamon
1 cup water	3 Tbsp. butter
½ cup beef (ground)	¼ cup pine nuts (roasted)
1 tsp. salt	1 roasting chicken (whole)
¼ tsp. pepper	½ cup water

Set oven at 400°F. Wash and drain rice. Place rice and water in saucepan. Cover and simmer for 15 minutes so rice will be partially cooked. Remove from heat. Add meat, salt, pepper, cinnamon, butter and pine nuts. Mix well. Set aside.

Wash and clean chicken thoroughly. Fill inside of cavity with stuffing. (If filling is too hot, spoon in the filling.) Add water to bottom of roaster. Place in chicken. Sprinkle a dash of salt and pepper over the chicken. Cover and bake for 1½-2 hours, basting occasionally.

Serve with Spinach Salad (page 46), Stuffed Grapevine Leaves (page 73), pickles, fresh yogurt.

Barbequed Chicken

Djaj Mishwi

2 lbs. chicken breasts	2 Tbsp. olive oil
½ cup lemon juice	3 cloves garlic (crushed)
1½ tsp. salt	4 small onions (quartered)
½ tsp. pepper	2 large green peppers (cubed)

Cut chicken breasts into 1-1½" cubes. Set aside.

In a large mixing bowl combine lemon juice, salt, pepper, olive oil and garlic. Mix well. Add the chicken, onions and peppers. Marinate for 2 hours in refrigerator, turning chicken pieces over several times during this period.

Alternate chicken pieces, onions and peppers on skewers. Barbeque over charcoal, turning until chicken is cooked.

Serve with Hommous bi Tahini (page 21), Tabouli (page 43), Yogurt, or Cucumber Salad (page 122).

VARIATION FOR BARBEQUING:
Use the chicken breasts whole. Marinate in lemon juice, salt, pepper, olive oil and garlic for 2 hrs. Barbeque over charcoal, turning once.

Chicken with Bread

Mousakhan

½ recipe Savory Pie Dough (page 134)	1½ tsp. salt
1 chicken (cut up)	½ tsp. pepper
2 large onions (finely chopped)	½ cup pine nuts
1½ cups sumac	2 Tbsp. butter
3 Tbsp. olive oil	¼ cup parsley (chopped fine)

Prepare Savory Pie Dough recipe using the whole egg and starting with ½ cup water, then using additional water as required. Cover with a plastic sheet then with a tea towel. Set aside to rise for 30 minutes.

Meanwhile, wash the chicken. Mix the onions, sumac, olive oil, salt and pepper together and rub these ingredients all over the chicken pieces. Set aside until dough rises.

Preheat oven to 325°F.

Grease a 9 x 12 inch pan. Spread dough evenly to reach the edges of the pan. Place chicken pieces and the onion mixture over the dough. Bake for 1-1¼ hours, or until chicken is tender.

Sauté pine nuts in butter until golden brown. Remove from heat.

Use 2 lifters to ease the bread from the pan and place on a large platter. Garnish with parsley sprinkled over top.

To serve, cut bread into serving pieces with a piece of chicken over top and a tablespoon of pine nuts over the chicken.

VARIATION:
Omit the Savory Pie Dough. Bake chicken and onion mixture together in a greased baking pan following the method above. Serve with warmed-up Pita Bread.

Marinated Chicken

Djaj mah Khal

1 frying chicken (cut up)
¼ cup vegetable oil
2 large onions (julienned)
2 Tbsp. flour
½ cup white vinegar
2 cups tomato sauce

1 cup water
1½ tsp. salt
½ tsp. pepper
½ tsp. allspice
½ tsp. cinnamon

Fry chicken pieces in oil until golden brown (partially cook only). Remove pieces from skillet and place in baking pan. Add onions to the oil the chicken was fried in. Sauté until onions are barely limp. Remove from oil and spread on top of chicken pieces.

Sprinkle flour in the frying oil and blend. Add vinegar, tomato sauce and water. Pour over chicken. Sprinkle seasonings over top of the mixture. Cover and bake in 400°F oven for 1 hour or until chicken is tender.

Serve with Rice Pilaf (page 112) and Cauliflower Salad (page 46).

Lemon Chicken

Djaj Mtabbel

1 cup lemon juice
3 cloves garlic (crushed)
1 tsp. salt
¼ tsp. pepper

1 tsp. basil
¼ tsp. cayenne
1 frying chicken (cut up)

Combine all ingredients in large mixing bowl, coating chicken pieces well. Marinate in refrigerator for 2-3 hours, turning chicken over several times during this period. Heat oven to 450°F. Place chicken in baking pan. Bake for 1 hour in the marinating mixture, basting occasionally. Remove chicken pieces onto a serving dish. Pour marinade over chicken pieces.

Serve with Tabouli (page 43), Zucchini-Potato Stew (page 62), Rice Pilaf (page 112).

VARIATION:
After chicken has marinated, place pieces on barbeque grill cooking one side, then turning over to cook the other side.

Mlukhiyyi with Chicken or Lamb

Mlukhiyyi bi Djaj awe Laham

Mlukhiyyi is a long leafy vegetable grown in a very hot climate. This vegetable is rarely found in North America. It may be found in dry form in Middle Eastern grocery stores.

1 lb. mlukhiyyi dry, or 2 lbs. fresh (If dry, soak in boiling water 1 hour.)
¼ cup vegetable oil
1 frying chicken (cut up), or 2 lbs. lamb shoulder cut into 1 inch cubes
    boiling water
¼ cup butter
2 large onions (finely chopped)
3 cloves garlic (crushed)
2 tsp. salt
½ tsp. pepper
1 lemon (cut in half)

Drain mlukhiyyi in colander. Place oil in large saucepan over medium heat. Fry chicken or lamb until golden brown, turning several times (do not cook through).

Add drained mlukhiyyi and stir. Cook for 3-4 minutes, stirring occasionally.

Add enough boiling water to cover the mixture. Turn heat to low, cover and cook for 30 minutes or until leaves and meat are tender.

Place butter, onions and garlic in skillet and sauté until golden brown. Add to mlukhiyyi mixture, add seasonings and cook for a further 5 minutes. Remove from heat.

Serve hot over Rice Pilaf (page 112). Squeeze lemon juice over individual servings.

Stuffed Turkey

Habash Mahshi

8-10 lb. turkey	2 tsp. salt (or to taste)
salt, pepper and allspice	1 tsp. nutmeg
½ cup pine nuts	½ tsp. pepper
3 Tbsp. butter	½ tsp. cinnamon
2 cups beef or lamb (coarsely ground)	2 cups water
turkey giblets (cut into small pieces)	¼ cup soft butter
2 cups long grain rice	3 cups water
(washed and drained)	chopped parsley

Wash turkey. Sprinkle a ½ teaspoon of each of the following; salt, pepper and allspice, inside and out. Set aside.

Sauté pine nuts in butter until nuts are golden brown. Add meat and giblets and sauté until meat changes color, then add rice and seasonings. Sauté for 1 minute. Add water. Bring to boil, cover and simmer for 15-20 minutes (rice should be partially cooked).

Spoon filling into turkey cavity. Close opening with skewers or sew with a needle and thread. Rub ¼ cup soft butter all over turkey. Set oven at 325°F.

Place turkey on rack in large roasting pan. Add 3 cups water to bottom of pan. Cover with lid or foil.

Bake for approximately 4 hours or until turkey meat is tender. Baste occasionally. Uncover for the last 30 minutes of baking time.

To serve, place on large platter. Remove thread or skewers from the turkey. Garnish with parsley.

Stuffing may be served separately on another platter.

This stuffing is also delicious for stuffing a large chicken, using one-half of the stuffing recipe.

Fish

In Lebanon fish dishes are always served with freshly squeezed lemon juice. Fish can also be soaked in lemon juice before cooking. Although fresh fish is best to work with, frozen may be substituted.

The recipes in this section involve many different cooking techniques. However, fish is always served with Sesame Seed Sauce or Pine Nut Sauce. Pieces of Pita Bread can be fried in the same oil as the fish which creates a tantalizing addition.

The rice and fish recipes together have an excellent flavor. The Stuffed Peppered Fish and the Baked Fish in Sesame Sauce are two favorites to be remembered. When a recipe in this section calls for fish, any white fish is suitable.

Top — *Stuffed Peppered Fish*
Bottom — *Salmon Steaks*

Cooking Guideline

Measure fish at thickest part. Allow 10 minutes per inch thickness for fresh or thawed fish, and 15-20 minutes per inch thickness for frozen fish.

Whenever possible, choose fillets, steaks or whole fish of a similar thickness for a more uniform cooking time.

To test for doneness, prod fish at thickest part with a fork; when cooked, the flesh should be opaque and flake or separate easily.

Do Not Overcook.

Stuffed Peppered Fish

Samak Harr

1 whole white fish (3-4 lbs.)
2 tsp. salt
½ cup peanut or vegetable oil
2 medium onions (finely chopped)
1 medium green pepper
(finely chopped)
1 medium red pepper (finely chopped)

2 tsp. hot pepper
(finely chopped) (optional)
¾ cup walnuts (finely chopped)
1 cup parsley (finely chopped)
1 lemon (sliced thick)

Clean and salt fish. Refrigerate for 1 hour.

Set oven at 400°F.

Pour half of the oil in a baking dish. Place fish in dish and turn over several times to ensure fish is coated with oil. Set aside for 20 minutes.

Heat remainder of oil in a heavy frying pan. Add onions and cook until golden brown. Stir in the peppers and walnuts. Sauté for 1 minute. Turn off heat. Add parsley.

While fish is still in baking dish, fill the cavity with the nut mixture. Close the opening with skewers or tooth picks and wrap kitchen string around a few times to secure.

Bake for 50-60 minutes, basting every 15 minutes. When fish is cooked remove string and tooth picks. Garnish with lemon slices and a few sprigs of parsley.

Serve hot or cold.

VARIATION:
Make Sesame Seed Sauce (page 26) and pour over baked fish.

Salmon Steaks and Vegetables

Samak mah Khodra

2 lbs. salmon steaks	**1 cup fresh mushrooms (sliced)**
¼ cup butter	**¼ tsp. pepper**
1 clove garlic (crushed)	**1 tsp. salt**
1 green pepper (sliced)	**1 tsp. oregano**
1 medium onion (sliced)	**1 Tbsp. dry parsley flakes**

Melt butter in a heavy skillet. Add salmon steaks. Fry for 3 minutes on one side and turn over. Add remaining ingredients, stirring gently until vegetables are limp but still crisp.

Serve with Rice for Fish (page 94), Chick Pea Dip (page 21).

Rice and Fish Platter

Samak mah Ruz

4 lbs. whole red or white snapper	**4 medium onions (sliced in rings)**
salt	**1½ cups long grain rice**
pepper	**1½ tsp. salt**
¼ tsp. cayenne	**1 tsp. pepper**
3 Tbsp. vegetable oil	**3 cups boiling water**
¼ cup parsley (coarsely chopped)	**lettuce leaves**
½ cup vegetable oil	**parsley sprigs**

Scale and clean the fish. Sprinkle with salt, pepper and cayenne. Drizzle 3 tablespoons oil all over the fish. Place parsley inside the cavity. Wrap fish in aluminum foil. Bake at 450 °F for 40-50 minutes.

Place the ½ cup vegetable oil in a saucepan. Add onions and fry on medium heat until onions are golden brown. Wash and drain rice, add to onion mixture, add salt and pepper and water, bring to boil. Turn to simmer, cover and cook for 20-25 minutes.

Lay lettuce leaves on a platter. Spoon the rice over the leaves. Place the fish over the rice. Spoon fish liquid that has formed over the fish.

Garnish with lemon slices and parsley sprigs.

Serve with Lebanese Salad (page 41).

Fried Fish

Samak Makli

2 medium white fish or 1 large (4 lbs.)
1 cup vegetable oil
3 tsp. salt
  flour (optional)

Clean fish and rinse with cold water. Sprinkle salt in cavity and over the outside of fish. Cut into serving pieces. Refrigerate for 1 hour then let stand at room temperature before frying.

Heat oil in skillet for frying. Flour fish lightly. When fish is cooked on one side, turn over and cook other side. Remove from skillet and drain on paper towels. Garnish fish with lemon wedges and parsley.

Serve with Sesame Seed Sauce (page 26) and Pita Bread torn into pieces and fried in the fish oil until lightly browned.

Fish in Garlic Sauce

Samak mah Tume

2 lbs. smelts
2 tsp. salt
½ tsp. pepper
  flour

½ cup vegetable oil
3 cloves garlic (crushed)
3 Tbsp. butter
¼ cup lemon juice

Clean smelts and remove all heads. Sprinkle with salt and pepper and coat with flour.

Heat vegetable oil in skillet. Add floured fish and fry until golden brown. Remove from oil, drain on paper towels and place on a serving platter.

Fry the garlic in butter until golden brown. Add the lemon juice and drizzle over the fish.

Serve warm or cold with Pita Bread and fresh vegetables.

Rice for Fish

Ruz la Samak

½ cup peanut or vegetable oil
¼ cup pine nuts
1 cup onions (sliced)
2 cups rice (washed and drained)

1 tsp. salt
¼ tsp. pepper
3½ cups boiling water

Heat oil in saucepan. Add pine nuts and brown lightly. Remove pine nuts from oil and set aside.

Lightly brown the onions in the same oil. Add rice, salt and pepper. Mix well. Add boiling water to rice. Bring to boil, cover and simmer until water has evaporated and rice is tender (approximately 30 minutes).

To serve: Turn out on platter and sprinkle with pine nuts. Garnish with fish pieces.

Fisherman's Plate

Sayadyia

1 fish (2-3 lbs. – preferably white)
½ cup vegetable oil
1 large onion (coarsely chopped)
1 cup walnut pieces

1 cup rice (washed and drained)
1½ tsp. salt
½ tsp. pepper
1½ cups water

Clean and salt fish.

Fry fish in the oil. Remove from frying pan and de-bone. Set aside.

Place oil from fish in a saucepan. Add onions and nuts and sauté until golden brown. Add rice, salt and pepper and sauté for 1 minute. Add fish pieces and water. Stir lightly. Bring to a boil. Cover and simmer for 30 minutes.

Remove gently from pot and place on a platter. Garnish with parsley sprigs and lemon wedges.

Serve with Fried Cauliflower (page 115) and salads.

Fish with Spinach

Samak bi Sabanikh

3-4 lbs. salmon or white fish
2 tsp. fresh sage *or*
1 tsp. dry sage
5 stalks celery
2 bunches fresh spinach
  (washed and drained)
1 cup green onions (chopped)

1 cup parsley
  (coarsely chopped)
1½ tsp. salt
½ tsp. pepper
¼ cup vegetable oil
½ cup water
⅔ cup fresh lemon juice

Clean fish and rub sage inside the cavity. Place in a baking dish.

Cut celery into 2 inch lengths and place over the fish. Cut spinach into bite size pieces and place over the celery. Add onion, parsley and seasonings. Drizzle the oil and water over the vegetables.

Bake at 425°F. for 30 minutes. Remove from oven and stir vegetables slightly. Add lemon juice, return to oven and bake for an additional 10 minutes.

Serve fish on large platter surrounded by the vegetables.

Baked Fish

Samak bil Furn

Any type of fish may be used.

1 whole fish (2-3 lbs.)
1½ tsp. salt
1 clove garlic (crushed)
2 Tbsp. butter
¼ tsp. pepper

¼ tsp. cayenne pepper
10 cherry tomatoes
6 lemon wedges
parsley sprigs

Clean and salt fish. Cover and place in refrigerator for 1 hour.

Heat oven to 400°F.

Place fish in baking dish in which it can be served.

Mix together the garlic, butter, pepper and cayenne, and rub inside the cavity and out. Bake for 40 minutes.

Remove from oven. Garnish with tomatoes, lemon wedges and a few parsley sprigs.

Serve with Sesame Seed Sauce (page 26), Baba Ghannuj (page 22).

Fish and Potato Casserole

Samak mah Batata

¼ cup vegetable oil	¼ cup fresh lemon juice
4 cloves garlic (crushed)	2 lbs. fish fillets
1½ tsp. salt	3 large potatoes
¼ tsp. pepper	2 large carrots
1 tsp. cumin	2 large tomatoes

Combine oil, garlic, salt, pepper and cumin in a baking dish. Add lemon juice.

Heat oven to 375°F.

Arrange fish in baking dish. Peel potatoes and cut them into ¼ inch slices. Cut carrots into thin strips. Slice tomatoes into ¼ inch slices. Arrange all vegetables around the fish.

Cover and bake for 30-40 minutes.

Serve hot with Pine Nut Sauce (page 27).

Barbequed Fish

Samak Mishwi

4 small fish	2 tsp. salt
½ cup lemon juice	¼ tsp. pepper
2 cloves garlic (crushed)	2 Tbsp. vegetable oil

Clean fish. Combine all remaining ingredients in a small bowl and pour over fish. Marinate for 1 hour in refrigerator, turning several times. Barbeque over charcoal until cooked. Allow 10 minutes cooking time per inch of thickness of fish.

May be served with Hommous bi Tahini (page 21), Tabouli (page 43).

Baked Fish in Sesame Sauce

Samak bi Taratour

A delightfully tangy flavor.

1 fish (approximately 2 lbs.) *or*	**¼ tsp. pepper**
4 fish steaks	**1 Sesame Seed Sauce recipe**
1 tsp. salt	**(page 26)**
½ cup vegetable oil	**parsley sprigs**
4 potatoes (peeled and sliced)	**lemon wedges**

Heat oven to 500°F.

Clean and salt fish.

Heat oil in skillet and fry fish until done. Remove and place in baking dish.

Fry potatoes in the same oil and place over the fish. Sprinkle pepper over top.

Pour Sesame Seed Sauce over the potatoes and fish. Place in oven and bake until sauce bubbles. Garnish with parsley sprigs and lemon wedges.

Serve with Fried Cauliflower (page 115).

Marinated Fish Fillets

Samak bi Khal

2 lbs. white fish fillets	**½ tsp. pepper**
1 cup olive oil	**1 tsp. dry sage**
⅔ cup vinegar	**2 Tbsp. parsley (finely chopped)**
¼ tsp. cayenne	**1 egg (well beaten)**
1½ tsp. salt	

Place fish in a mixing bowl with olive oil and vinegar. Refrigerate in marinade for 2 hours.

Set oven at 450°F.

Drain and place fish in a buttered baking dish. Sprinkle with seasonings. Add parsley to beaten egg and pour over the fish. Bake for 10-15 minutes.

Serve with fresh vegetables and lemon wedges.

Burghul
(Crushed Wheat)

To make burghul, the whole wheat kernels are boiled, dried, then crushed. This crushed wheat is divided into three different sizes. The fine powder form may be used to flour the board when making bread. The regular or medium size is a basic ingredient of Lebanese dishes such as Kibbi and Tabouli, two of the most popular Lebanese recipes. The coarse burghul is found in pilaf dishes, soups, stews and Saffi.

The fine powder size is not used in this section.

The most popular, the regular or medium size, is identified in the following recipes as crushed wheat or burghul. Some recipes call for coarse crushed wheat and this distinction will be clearly indicated.

Burghul is sometimes called "bulgar" and when mixed with flour, becomes a meatless dish. However, when combined with meat, a variety of gourmet dishes and hors d'oeuvres result.

It should be noted that crushed wheat is not the same as cracked wheat; cracked wheat has not been boiled before crushing.

Top — *Kibbi Balls, Fresh Yogurt*
Centre — *Burghul Balls in Lemon Sauce*
Bottom — *Kibbi Nayii*

Kibbi Balls

Kibbi Makliya

Kibbi is one of the most versatile of the Lebanese foods. It may be made in many different sizes and shapes, hot or cold. Serve as an appetizer, as a main course, or as a unique picnic food.

½ Kibbi Nayii recipe (page 103)
1 Kibbi Filling recipe (page 105)
vegetable oil for frying

Prepare Kibbi Nayii and the filling. With wet hands, take a small piece of Kibbi. Make a ball the size of a walnut from the mixture. With the ball in one hand, mould with forefinger of other hand, rotating the ball evenly to make the hole larger until you have a thin shell. If you make a break in the shell, patch with a bit of the mixture.

Fill the hollow with the filling. Close the ball by bringing the open end of the kibbi ball together using a little water on finger tips. Shape should resemble a sphere.

Place on cookie sheet until all kibbi spheres are completed. Deep fry until golden brown. Remove from oil, drain on paper towels. Serve hot or cold.

Serve with salads, cold Yogurt (page 123), Baba Ghannuj (page 22), or Tabouli (page 43).

VARIATION:
(1) Make larger spheres by making a ball the size of an egg filling the cavity. Add these spheres to boiling Kishk Soup (page 35). Cook for 10 minutes.
(2) Add Kibbi spheres to boiling cooked Yogurt Soup (page 126). Cook for 10 minutes.
(3) To make Kibbi patties, make a cavity in the ball, fill, close, and flatten into a pattie. Smooth using a little water. Deep fry. Kibbi spheres or patties may also be broiled or barbequed.

Burghul Balls in Lemon Sauce

Zonkol bi Limoon   Meatless

This soup dish may be served for lunch as a meal in itself.

½ cup dry chick peas (soaked overnight)   1 medium onion
8 cups water   (finely chopped)
1 recipe Meatless Kibbi (page 104)   ½ cup vegetable oil
2 tsp. salt (or to taste)   ½ cup lemon juice
½ tsp. pepper   2 Tbsp. sumac (optional)
1 clove garlic (crushed)

Drain chick peas. In large saucepan combine chick peas and water. Cover and cook until peas are tender.

While peas are cooking, prepare meatless kibbi and form into small balls the size of marbles. Place on cookie sheet until all of the mixture has been used. Add to chick pea mixture. Add salt, pepper and garlic and simmer over low heat.

Sauté onions with oil in a frying pan until golden brown. Add to chick pea mixture. Add lemon juice and sumac. Cover and cook for 30 minutes over low heat at a steady boil.

Baked Kibbi

Kibbi bi Saneah

May be served as an appetizer.

1 Kibbi Nayii recipe (page 103) add ½ cup burghul
1 Kibbi Filling recipe (page 105)
¼ cup melted butter

Prepare the Kibbi Nayii and the Kibbi Filling. Heat oven to 375°F.

Butter a 9 x 12 inch cake pan. Spread half of the Kibbi Nayii recipe on the bottom of the pan, patting evenly with wet hands. Spread the Filling over the layer. Spread the other half of the Kibbi over the Filling.

It may be easier to make small patties and lay them over the top of the filling. Patch up and smooth over with wet hands. Cut into 2 inch squares or any desired shape.

Pour melted butter over top. Bake for 45-60 minutes, or until cooked through (do not overcook).

Serve with Lebanese Salad (page 41), Stuffed Tomatoes (page 72), or inside a Pita pocket with pickles.

Kibbi

Kibbi Nayii

"The National Dish of Lebanon"

Burghul is a natural source of fibre and is an excellent source of protein. It is essential to the Lebanese diet.

It is best to grind your own lean meat from a fresh leg of lamb or a beef roast. This dish is served raw. In Lebanon, some still pound the meat in a heavy stone or marble Mortar called Jorn, using a heavy pestle. Most people today use an electric meat grinder or food processor.

2 cups crushed wheat (burghul)	**1 ½ tsp. salt (or to taste)**
4 cups ice cold water	**½ tsp. pepper**
2 lbs. very lean beef or lamb (ground)	**½ tsp. allspice (optional)**
1 medium onion (grated fine)	

Place crushed wheat in large mixing bowl and add water. Let stand 5 minutes and drain, squeezing out water.

Add ground meat, onion and seasonings. Mix well. If not pliable, add a little cold water.

Run the mixture through a meat grinder twice using fine holes (if using a food processor, process in 2 lots for 30 seconds each). Mix again.

Place on platter and shape into a flat round. Dip hands into cold water and smooth all over. Using a fork or spoon, decorate the kibbi by pressing very lightly. Garnish with parsley sprigs.

Serve with green onions, pickles, olive oil, Tabouli (page 43), Green Bean Stew (page 61).

VARIATION:
This is the basic Kibbi Nayii recipe and can also be used for:
(1) Kibbi Balls (page 101)
(2) Baked Kibbi (page 102)
(3) When using Kibbi for a cooked recipe, use an additional ½ cup of crushed wheat.

Meatless Kibbi

Kibbi Tahili

1½ cups crushed wheat (burghul)   ½ cup flour
2 cups warm water   1 Kibbi Filling recipe (page 105)
1 tsp. salt   oil for frying
   dash of pepper

Soak wheat in water for 2 minutes. Drain slightly. Add salt, pepper and flour. Knead well. If required, add a little warm water to the mixture. Should be consistency of pie dough.

Shape mixture into spheres or patties. Follow the same method used for Kibbi Balls (page 101) using the Kibbi Filling recipe.

VARIATION:
(1) Gently drop balls into boiling Yogurt Soup (page 126) or Kishk Soup (page 35).
(2) Make marble sized balls from the mixture. Place them on a cookie sheet until all have been rolled. Drop into boiling soup. Cook for 10-15 minutes.

Burghul and Chick Peas

Burghul mah Hommous

1 cup ground beef or Meat Reserve   1 cup coarse crushed wheat
   (Awarma – page 62)   1½ tsp salt (or to taste)
1 medium onion (coarsely chopped)   ¼ tsp. pepper
8 cups water   (or to taste)
½ cup chick peas (soaked overnight)

Sauté meat and onion in saucepan until meat is lightly browned. Add water and chick peas. Bring to boil over high heat. Lower heat and cook until chick peas are tender. Add coarse crushed wheat and seasonings and cook for an additional 15-20 minutes, stirring occasionally.

This dish resembles a thick soup and should be eaten with a spoon.

VARIATION:
Substitute ½ pound beef or lamb ribs for ground meat. Brown ribs and onion with 3 tablespoons vegetable oil. Add water and chick peas, following instructions in above recipe.

Potato Kibbi

Kibbit Batata

4 **medium potatoes**	¼ **tsp. pepper**
(boiled then peeled)	1 **cup Meat Reserve**
1 **cup crushed wheat (burghul)**	**(Awarma – page 62)** *or*
2 **heaping Tbsp. flour**	½ **Kibbi Filling recipe (page 105)**
1½ **tsp. salt**	¼ **cup vegetable oil for frying**

If using meat reserve for filling, add ½ cup walnuts or pine nuts.

Place potatoes and dry crushed wheat in mixing bowl. Mash potatoes with the crushed wheat. Add flour, salt and pepper. Knead well. If needed, add a few drops of water (should be consistency of pie dough).

Roll some of the mixture into a ball the size of an egg. Make a large cavity in the centre, put in filling, close and pat down into a pattie. Smooth all over with dampened hands. Set aside until all patties have been shaped. Pan fry both sides in a skillet with the vegetable oil.

Serve with salads, Hommous bi Tahini (page 21), Baked Kafta (page 52).

Kibbi Filling

Hashwat Kibbi

½ **cup pine nuts or walnuts**	½ **cup parsley (finely chopped)**
2 **Tbsp. butter**	¼ **tsp. pepper**
1 **lb. beef or lamb (ground)**	1 **tsp. salt**
1 **medium onion (finely chopped)**	¼ **tsp. allspice**

Sauté nuts with butter in a frying pan until golden brown. Add meat, onion, parsley and seasonings. Sauté until meat is brown and onions are limp. Cool slightly before using.

VARIATION:
Add ½ cup Yogurt Spread (page 124) to the filling.

Lamb with Burghul

Burghul bi Laham

1½ lbs. lamb stew meat (cut into
   2 inch cubes)
2 medium onions (quartered)
3 Tbsp. vegetable oil
3 cups water
1 cup coarse crushed wheat

1 19 oz. can chick peas
   (drained)
1½ tsp. salt (or to taste)
¼ tsp. pepper
½ tsp. cinnamon

Brown meat and onions in oil in large saucepan. Add water, cover and cook until meat is tender, removing the foam as it forms. Add approximately ½ cup water to replace evaporated liquid. Add coarse crushed wheat, chick peas and seasonings. Simmer until crushed wheat is cooked (approximately 30 minutes). This dish should be of pilaf consistency.

Serve with pickles and yogurt.

Burghul with Tomatoes

Burghul mah Banadoora

3 large ripe tomatoes *or*
¼ cup tomato paste
¾ cup lean ground beef *or*
   Meat Reserve (Awarma – page 62))
1 medium onion (coarsely chopped)

1½ cups coarse crushed wheat
7 cups water
1½ tsp. salt (or to taste)
¼ tsp. pepper

Remove skin from tomatoes, dice and set aside.

Combine meat and onion in saucepan. Sauté until onions are transparent. Add dry coarse crushed wheat and stir. Add tomatoes and remaining ingredients.

Bring to boil over medium-high heat. Lower heat to medium and cook for 20-25 minutes, stirring occasionally.

This dish resembles a stew.

Serve with pickles and salads.

Meatless Burghul Pilaf

Burghul M'falfal Bedoun Laham   Meatless

¼ cup butter
1½ cups coarse crushed wheat
1 tsp. salt

¼ tsp. pepper
3 cups water

Combine butter and crushed wheat in saucepan. Sauté on medium heat for 1 minute. Add seasonings, stir and add water. Bring to boil. Turn heat to low, cover and simmer for 20-25 minutes.

Crushed wheat should be fluffy and moist.

Serve as a substitute for Rice Pilaf.

VARIATION:
After adding the water place mixture in a casserole dish. Cover and bake in 350°F oven for 20 minutes. Stir gently and return to oven. Cover and bake for another 15 minutes.

Burghul Pilaf

Burghul M'falfal

1 cup ground beef *or*
  Meat Reserve (Awarma – page 62)
1 medium onion (coarsely chopped)
2 cups coarse crushed wheat

4 cups water
1½ tsp. salt (or to taste)
¼ tsp. pepper

Sauté meat and onion in saucepan until meat is slightly browned. Add dry coarse crushed wheat and stir immediately. Add water and seasonings. Bring to a boil. Lower heat to a steady low boil, cover and cook for 20-25 minutes, stirring occasionally.

Serve with pickles and fresh Yogurt.

Meatless Dishes

Vegetables and grains are the staples for those wishing to limit the amount of meat in the diet. The recipes in this section are both nutritious and filling. They are also easy to prepare and very economical.

Meatless dishes may be served as an accompaniment to Kibbi, yogurt, Savory Pastries and salads. Rice Pilaf is excellent with stews. Meatless dishes can even be served as hot or cold appetizers.

There are numerous meatless recipes found throughout this book, but the majority of vegetable and lenten dishes can be found in this section.

Top — *Broad Beans and Eggs*
Centre — *Potato Omelet*
Bottom — *Okra*

Broad Beans and Eggs

Fool mah Bayd

Green broad beans or fava beans may be purchased from supermarkets in cans, from specialty food stores freshly frozen, or fresh from the garden using the beans inside the pod. Whole tender beans with the pod may be substituted. String and cut beans into 1½ inch lengths.

1 medium onion (coarsely chopped)	½ tsp. cumin
¼ cup butter	1 tsp. salt
4 cups green broad beans (fava beans)	¼ tsp. pepper
¼ cup water	4 eggs

Sauté onions in butter until onions are limp. Add beans and stir; fry for 2 minutes on medium heat.

Add water and cover with lid. Cook over medium-low heat for approximately 20-25 minutes until beans are tender.

Add seasonings. Break eggs and add to bean mixture, stirring slightly to break the yolk. Cook only until eggs are set.

Serve with Pita Bread, sliced tomatoes or Yogurt Cucumber Salad (page 122).

Potato Omelet

Ijjit Batata

4 large potatoes (peeled and shredded)	¼ tsp. pepper
1 medium onion (finely chopped)	4 eggs
3 Tbsp. flour	½ cup parsley (finely chopped)
1 tsp. salt	1½ cups vegetable oil (for frying)

Rinse shredded potatoes in cold water and squeeze out excess water. Place in mixing bowl. Add all remaining ingredients except vegetable oil. Mix well, but do not beat. Set aside.

Heat oil for frying. Drop a heaping tablespoon of the mixture into the oil (5 or 6 may be made at a time). Cook until golden brown on each side. Place on paper towel to drain.

If necessary, a little more oil may be added during the latter part of frying.

Serve with pickles and fresh vegetables inside Pita Bread pockets.

Okra

Bamyi

2 lbs. young okra (fresh or frozen)
¼ cup vegetable oil
1 medium onion (finely chopped)
2 cloves garlic (chopped)
½ Tbsp. coriander

salt and pepper to taste
1 cup tomato sauce
2 cups water
1 Rice Pilaf recipe (page 112)

Place oil and onion in saucepan and sauté for 2 minutes. Add all remaining ingredients. Bring to boil over high heat. Turn to low and cook for 25-30 minutes or until okra is tender.

While okra is cooking, prepare rice. Serve okra over rice.

VARIATION:
1 cup ground beef or Meat Reserve (Awarma, page 62) may be substituted for vegetable oil. Sauté meat with onions until onions are transparent. Proceed, adding the okra following above directions.

Rice Pilaf

Ruz M'falfal

½ cup vermicelli (cut into 1-2 inch pieces)
¼ cup butter (unsalted)
1½ cups rice (soaked in hot water for 1 hour)

1½ tsp. salt
2½ cups water

Brown vermicelli noodles in the butter in saucepan. Add drained rice, stirring over medium heat for 1 minute. Stir in salt and water. Turn to high heat and bring to a boil. Turn heat to simmer; cover and cook for 20-25 minutes or until rice is tender.

Serve with any stew dish and fresh yogurt.

NOTE:
If rice is not presoaked, wash and drain. Add an additional ½ cup water to above. Cooking time will be approximately 5-10 minutes longer.

Parsley Omelet

Ijjit Bakdunis

4 eggs
½ cup parsley (finely chopped)
2 Tbsp. flour
¼ tsp. salt

¼ tsp. pepper
¼ cup green onions (finely chopped) (optional)
3 Tbsp. butter

Combine all ingredients, except butter, mixing well (do not beat). Heat frying pan over medium heat, add butter. Pour in the egg mixture. While omelet is cooking, lift up edges for some of the egg to seep through. Cook until lightly brown. Flip over to cook the other side.

Serve with pickles and raw vegetables, or fill inside a Pita pocket.

Zucchini Omelet

Ijjit Koosa

3 zucchini, 6-7 inches long, grated
   or the pulp from Stuffed
   Zucchini recipe (page 71)
4 eggs
3 Tbsp. flour

1 tsp. salt
½ tsp. pepper
¼ cup green onions (finely chopped)
¼ cup parsley (finely chopped)
1½ cups oil (for frying)

Rinse the grated zucchini or vegetable marrow. Squeeze all the water out using both hands; place in mixing bowl. Add remaining ingredients, except oil, and mix (do not beat).

Heat oil for frying. Using a large tablespoon, drop mixture into hot oil getting as many patties as possible in the frying pan at a time. Turn over when one side is golden brown and cook the other side. Remove from oil and drain on paper towels.

These mini omelets can be served with pickles inside Pita Bread or may be made larger and served with bacon or ham for lunch.

Fried Vegetables

Khodra Makala

¼ cup vegetable oil	2 zucchini (sliced)
1 medium onion (julienned)	1½ tsp. salt
3 medium potatoes (diced small)	¼ tsp. pepper

Place vegetable oil in large skillet. Add onions and sauté for 1 minute over medium heat.

Add potatoes and sauté for 5 minutes.

Add zucchini and seasonings. Stir gently and cook until vegetables are tender, stirring occasionally.

Serve with fresh yogurt or salads.

VARIATION:
½ cup Meat Reserve (Awarma) may be substituted for the vegetable oil.

Fried Eggplant

Bitinjan Makli

2 large eggplant
  salt
1 cup vegetable oil (for frying)

Peel eggplant, cut into ½ inch thick slices and sprinkle salt on both sides. Spread out on paper towels to drain for 30 minutes.

Heat oil for frying. Fry on both sides until golden brown.

Drain on paper towels.

Serve as a side dish with any meal.

Fried Cauliflower

Karnabeet Makli

1 medium cauliflower	1 tsp. salt
2 eggs	¼ tsp. pepper
2 Tbsp. flour	1½ cups oil (for frying)

Cut cauliflower into flowerettes and parboil. Drain, set aside.

Slightly beat eggs, with flour, salt and pepper. Heat oil in skillet. Dip each flowerette into the egg mixture. Fry in the oil until golden brown. Place on paper towel to drain.

Can be used as a side dish with any meal, or as an appetizer.

Broad Bean Fry

Fool Makala

2 lbs. whole, tender broad beans	¼ cup vegetable oil
1 medium onion (chopped)	1 tsp. coriander powder
2 cloves garlic (crushed)	¾ cup water
salt and pepper to taste	½ cup lemon juice
⅛ tsp. allspice	

Wash beans, removing string from edges. Cut into 1½ inch lengths. Place beans in cold water so they will not turn dark. Set aside.

Sauté onions, garlic, salt, pepper and allspice in oil until onions are lightly browned. Add coriander to onion mixture. Sauté for another minute.

Add drained beans, tossing thoroughly. Cook and stir for 3 minutes. Add water, cover and cook for 25 minutes or until beans are tender.

Add lemon juice and simmer for 10 minutes.

Serve with Rice Pilaf (page 112), Fried Cauliflower (page 115), or Fried Eggplant (page 114).

Serves 4-6.

Eggplant-Chick Pea Stew

Bitinjan mah Hommous

1 large onion (coarsely chopped)	1½ tsp. salt
½ cup vegetable oil	¼ tsp. pepper
½ cup dry chick peas (soaked overnight)	¼ tsp. cinnamon
3 cups water	4 large, ripe tomatoes (diced)
1 large eggplant	*or* ¼ cup tomato paste

Place onions and oil in saucepan. Cook until onions are golden brown. Add drained chick peas and water. Cook until peas are tender (approximately 30 minutes).

Peel eggplant and cut into 1 inch cubes. Add to chick pea mixture. Add seasonings and diced tomatoes. If tomato paste is used add ½ cup water to mixture. Cover and cook for 20-25 minutes on medium heat, stirring occasionally until eggplant is tender.

May be served hot or cold.

Serve with Rice Pilaf (page 112).

Lentils with Rice

Moujadara

1½ cups dry lentils (washed and drained)	½ cup rice (washed and drained)
8 cups water	
1½ tsp. salt	½ cup vegetable oil
¼ tsp. pepper	1 medium onion (julienned)

Wash lentils, drain and place in saucepan. Add water. Cover and cook for 1 hour or until lentils are tender.

Add salt, pepper and rice to the lentils. Cook at a steady boil on low heat for 25 minutes, stirring occasionally.

Sauté onions in oil until onions are golden brown. Add to cooking lentil mixture, stir and remove from heat.

Serve hot or cold with fresh cold yogurt, Lebanese Salad (page 41), pickles and a squeeze of lemon over each individual serving.

VARIATIONS:
(1) 1 cup rice may be substituted for the ½ cup rice in recipe above. This will make the recipe thicker.
(2) 1 cup coarse crushed wheat may be substituted for rice.

Zucchini Casserole

Koosa Matboukh

4 zucchini (8-9 inches long)
3 cloves garlic (crushed)
2 Tbsp. fresh *or* 1 Tbsp. dry mint
¼ cup vegetable oil

1 tsp. salt
¼ tsp. pepper
½ cup water

Set oven at 375°F.

Wash zucchini and cut into ½ inch slices. Place in a casserole dish. Combine sauce ingredients; garlic, mint, oil, salt, pepper and water. Pour sauce over the zucchini. Cover and bake for 40-45 minutes, or until zucchini is tender.

Serve with fresh cold yogurt.

Spinach with Rice

Ruz bi Sabanikh

1 medium onion (coarsely)
½ cup vegetable oil
1 tsp. salt
¼ tsp. pepper

1 bunch fresh spinach
2½ cups water
1 cup rice
lemon wedges

Place onions, oil and seasonings in a saucepan. Sauté until golden brown.

Wash spinach well and drain. Chop into 2-3 inch pieces. Add spinach to onion mixture, cover and cook until spinach is limp. Add water and rice. Do not stir. Bring to boil on medium heat to simmer, cover and cook for 25 minutes.

Serve with a squeeze of lemon for each serving.

Yogurt Dishes
(Laban)

Yogurt has been called a "wonder food" by many. Only two ingredients are needed to make it — milk and culture (starter). It may be made with milk from a variety of animals, resulting in different flavors and consistencies.

Yogurt has been consumed in the Middle East for centuries, making it the most ancient processed food known. This wonder food has been called a natural antibiotic; a cup of yogurt a day keeps the digestive system healthy as this is utilized by the body twice as fast as milk.

The recipe for homemade yogurt in this section uses whole milk, although skim milk may be substituted for calorie restricted diets. Yogurt easily replaces sour cream not only on baked potatoes but in many other dishes as well.

Always save some yogurt as it can be used as the starter for your next batch.

Commercially made yogurt may be substituted in any recipe in this section.

Top — *Meat Pastries in Yogurt Soup*
Centre — *Yogurt Cucumber Salad*
Bottom — *Yogurt Eggplant Puree*

Yogurt Cucumber Salad

Khiar bi Laban   Meatless

1 clove garlic	1 long English cucumber
1 tsp. salt	1 Tbsp. mint leaves (chopped)
2 cups Yogurt (page 123)	*or* ½ Tbsp. dry mint

Crush garlic with salt in a salad bowl. Blend in yogurt. Slice through the length of the cucumber, then chop into thin slices. Add to yogurt mixture. Mix gently. Sprinkle the mint over top to garnish.

Serve with any Kibbi dishes, Savory Pastries, or Omelets.

Yogurt-Eggplant Puree

Laban mah Bitinjan   Meatless

1 large eggplant	2 cloves garlic (crushed)
3 Tbsp. lemon juice	salt and pepper to taste
2 Tbsp. olive oil	2 Tbsp. parsley (finely
¾ cup Yogurt (page 123)	chopped)

Remove stem end from eggplant. Pierce the skin several times with a fork. Place in 400°F oven in a baking dish or cook over charcoal until eggplant is soft.

While eggplant is still hot, run under cold water then remove skin.

Place in serving bowl and add all remaining ingredients, except parsley. Mash with potato masher.

For a finer texture, place all ingredients in food processor or blender. Blend until smooth.

Garnish with parsley.

To serve: Use as a dip for Pita Bread, serve with meat dishes or as an appetizer.

Yogurt
Laban   Meatless

Yogurt is one of the staples in any Lebanese home, made in various consistencies.

2 quarts whole milk
2 Tbsp. yogurt starter (rawbi)

Place milk in a heavy saucepan (not aluminum) over medium heat. Bring to boil, being careful not to let milk scorch (no need to stir).

Remove from heat and let cool until lukewarm. Milk is ready if you can count to ten comfortably when you immerse your little finger into the milk.

If milk is too cool return to heat and warm slightly, if too hot leave aside for a while longer to cool down. Place yogurt starter in a cup (this can be from starter saved from the last time you made yogurt or plain yogurt which is commercially made) and add approximately 4 Tbsp. of warm milk. Blend together and add to the rest of the warm milk. Stir well.

Yogurt mixture may be left in the same pot to set. Cover with a lid and a heavy blanket. Place in a spot where mixture will not be disturbed for 5-6 hours, or until set.

Place in refrigerator to cool. Taste will vary according to age of starter.

Serve cold with Kibbi bi Saneah (page 102), Fatayer recipes and Rice Pilaf (page 112).

VARIATION:
Skim milk may be substituted for whole milk.

Burghul Balls in Cold Yogurt
Zonkol bi Laban   Meatless

1 Meatless Kibbi recipe (page 104)   **1 tsp. salt**
5 cups water   **5-6 cups cold Yogurt (page 123)**
  dash of salt   **2 Tbsp. fresh mint** *or* **1 Tbsp. dry**
2 cloves garlic (crushed)

Shape meatless kibbi into small marbles. Set aside. Place water in saucepan and add a dash of salt. Bring to boil. Add the burghul balls and cook for 15-20 minutes at a steady low boil. Drain and set aside.

Combine the garlic, salt and yogurt together in a serving bowl. Blend thoroughly with a fork. Add burghul balls and mix slightly. Sprinkle mint over top.

Serve chilled for lunch with Shish Kabob (page 51).

Yogurt Spread

Labani

1 Yogurt recipe (page 123)
2 tsp. salt

Pour the cold yogurt into a cloth or cheese cloth bag doubled in thickness and tied. Hang and let drain for 1 day.

Remove yogurt from bag and place in a mixing bowl. Add salt and mix well. Refrigerate in suitable covered container.

If desired, a sprinkle of olive oil may be spread on top of the yogurt spread. If only a small amount of yogurt spread is to be made, place fresh cold yogurt into a coffee filter and let drain into a container.

To serve, spread yogurt on Pita Bread, add a sprinkle of olive oil and dry mint and place under the broiler for 2 minutes.

Serve for breakfast or a snack with olives, eggs and Herb Bread (page 137).

Yogurt Balls

Labani Makbouse   Meatless

Preserved in oil, yogurt is an old standby for a snack spread on Pita Bread (Kmaj).

1 Yogurt recipe (page 123)
2 Tbsp. salt
olive oil

Pour the cold yogurt into a cloth or cheese cloth bag doubled in thickness. Tie and let hang to drain for 2 days until the yogurt becomes the consistency of cream cheese.

Remove yogurt from bag and place in a large bowl. Add salt. Mix well.

Make balls the size of a walnut, using a little oil on the palm of hands to prevent sticking. Place balls on clean tea towel or paper towel for approximately 2 hours to drain more of the moisture.

Drop into sterilized jars, cover with oil and seal.

To serve: Spread a yogurt ball and a teaspoon of the oil on Pita Bread and roll, or spread a ball of yogurt on Pita Bread adding a sprinkle of mint and warm in oven for 2 minutes.

Chick Peas and Yogurt

Hommous mah Laban   Meatless

1 19 oz. can chick peas (save half the liquid)   **1 cup plain yogurt**
2 cloves garlic   **2 Pita Bread loaves(toasted)**
½ tsp. salt   **¼ cup melted butter**

Place chick peas and half of the liquid in a sauce pan. Bring to boil, set aside.

In a mixing bowl mash garlic and salt together. Add hot chick peas and liquid, mixing thoroughly. Add yogurt mixing slightly.

Break bread into 1½ inch pieces. Place in salad bowl. Add chick pea and yogurt mixture. Do not mix. Drizzle butter over top.

Serve for breakfast or lunch.

Lamb with Yogurt

Laban Immu

2 lbs. lean lamb meat (cut into 1″ cubes)   **1 ⅓ cups water**
3-4 small whole onions   **2 Tbsp. dry mint**
1 egg (slightly beaten)   **2 cloves garlic (crushed)**
1 quart plain yogurt   **3 Tbsp. butter**

Place meat cubes in sauce pan with enough water to cover. Bring to a boil. Skim off foam, then turn heat to medium. Cover with lid. Cook for 20 minutes. Add whole peeled onions and continue cooking until meat is tender.

Yogurt mixture:

In a saucepan place beaten egg, yogurt and water. Mix well. Stir constantly in one direction over medium heat until yogurt comes to a boil. Pour this mixture over the meat and broth.

In a small saucepan sauté mint, garlic and butter. Pour over the meat and yogurt mixture.

Serve hot over Rice Pilaf (page 112).

125

Eggs in Yogurt Mint Sauce

Bayd bi Laban   Meatless

1 Yogurt Soup recipe (page 126)   **2 Tbsp. dry mint**
6 eggs   2 cloves garlic (crushed)
1 Tbsp. butter

Prepare Yogurt Soup recipe. When soup comes to a boil, turn down heat slightly. Break eggs, one at a time, and drop gently into the boiling soup (will be similar to poached eggs). Cook for 5 minutes.

In a small pan sauté butter, mint and garlic for 1 minute. Add to yogurt mixture. Remove from heat.

Serve for lunch, or as a soup entrée at dinner.

Yogurt Soup

Shourabit Laban   Meatless

4 cups Yogurt (page 123)   **1 egg**
4 cups water   **1½ tsp. salt**
½ cup rice   **mint (fresh or dry)**

Place yogurt in heavy saucepan. Beat with a fork until smooth. Add water and stir. Set aside.

Rinse and drain rice. Add egg and mix well. Add the rice and egg mixture to the yogurt along with the salt.

Place saucepan over medium heat, stirring constantly in one direction with a wooden spoon, being careful not to scorch. Bring to a boil. Turn down heat slightly and cook for 15-20 minutes stirring occasionally.

Serve hot or cold with a sprinkle of fresh or dry mint.

This yogurt soup is used for these recipes: Meat Pastries in Yogurt Soup (page 121), Eggs in Yogurt Mint Sauce (page 126).

VARIATION:
(1) Add Kibbi Balls (page 101) to the soup after it comes to a boil and cook for 15-20 minutes.
(2) Prepare Meatless Kibbi recipe (page 104), shape into marble size balls, and drop into the boiling soup. Cook for 15-20 minutes.
(3) Stuffed Zucchini (page 71) may be added to the soup at the same time the rice is added. Cook for 40-50 minutes or until rice inside zucchini is cooked.

Arabic Cheese

Jibin

1 gallon whole milk
1 tablet cheese rennet or junket tablet
pickling salt

Heat milk to lukewarm (a little cooler than yogurt recipe – page 123), on medium heat in heavy saucepan (not aluminum).

Crush the tablet to a powder in a cup and dissolve in 2 Tbsp. of cold water. Add to milk, stir well. Remove from heat.

Cover with lid, then a heavy blanket. Keep in a warm place where mixture will not be disturbed for 2-4 hours.

When mixture congeals, break up with hands to separate the curd from the liquid. Discard liquid.

Take some of the curd into both hands pressing lightly to drain out the liquid, forming a cheese pattie or, place a small amount of the curd in a fine sieve and press gently. Place on a platter to drain further.

If cheese is to be served fresh do not salt. To preserve, sprinkle a teaspoon of pickling salt on top of each pattie. Cover with clear film, refrigerate overnight.

Make a brine with 2 quarts water and ½ cup pickling salt. Bring to a boil, cool. If necessary, cut cheese patties in half or quarters to fit into jars. Pack cheese patties into sterilized jars, fill with brine and seal.

To serve: Soak the cheese in cold water for several hours to remove salt.

Serve for breakfast, lunch or snacks with Pita Bread. This cheese may also be used for the Cheese Bread recipe (page 137).

Savory Pastries and Breads

Filled savory pies are the ideal finger food. They may be served as a meal, snack or an appetizer. There is no limit as to what size or shape to create. The meat filled pies should be served warm, and the vegetable filled pies may be served warm or cold.

Savory pies will keep well refrigerated for several days (make a double batch and freeze). They may be warmed up for serving. The flavor and texture will return to freshly baked.

Talami is a thick round bread and is soft in texture. This bread does not have a pocket in it. It is excellent served with meals especially stews.

Pita Bread (Kmaj) is a round hollow crust evenly baked. Pita Bread should be baked in a very hot oven. This bread originated in the Holy Land, dating back to biblical times. When cut across the diameter it provides an instant pocket to fill with any type of food.

Top — *Pita Bread*
Centre — *Spinach Filled Fyllo*
Bottom — *Spinach Pies*

Pita Bread
Kmaj

This bread adapts very well to any type of food. It is served with every Lebanese meal. Tear a bite size piece from the Pita round, and use to pick up morsels of food from the plate.

2½ cups lukewarm water	½ tsp. salt
1 tsp. sugar	5½ cups flour (white or whole wheat)
3½ tsp. active dry yeast	

Place water and sugar in large bowl and stir. Add yeast and stir slightly. Let rest for 5 minutes.

Mix in salt and flour gradually, starting with 3½ cups flour then adding the rest. More or less water may be required, depending on the brand of the flour. Use enough flour to prevent dough from clinging to bowl. Knead well for 5 minutes. Place a little vegetable oil on palms of hands and smooth all over to prevent crusting. Cover with plastic sheet then tea towel and allow to rest for 20-30 minutes.

Set oven at 500°F.

Divide dough into 8 balls. Roll out each ball into ¼ inch in thickness. Let rest covered for 20 minutes on generously floured table or counter top.

Bake on greased cookie sheets for 5-8 minutes or until lightly browned. The higher the oven temperature the better the results.

May be kept in a plastic bag in the refrigerator for several days or may be frozen.

To warm Pita, place the round on the rack in the oven at 300°F for 1-2 minutes.

See section on Pita Bread fillings. Pita Bread is adapted to Western cooking with a touch of Lebanese.

Spinach Filled Fyllo

Sabanikh bi Ajeen Baklawa   Meatless

2 large bunches of spinach   ½ cup lemon juice
   (washed and drained)   ¼ cup vegetable oil
½ cup parsley (finely chopped)   ½ cup feta cheese
3 green onions (finely chopped)   1 lb. fyllo dough
1½ tsp. salt   soft butter
¼ tsp. pepper

If fyllo dough is frozen, thaw at room temperature for 4-5 hours. Unroll and cover with damp cloth. Handle fyllo carefully while working with it. Always keep remaining dough covered with a damp cloth.

Set oven at 350°F. Chop spinach into bite size pieces and place in large bowl. Add chopped parsley, onions, salt, pepper, lemon juice and vegetable oil. Chop up feta cheese and add to spinach mixture. Toss well.

Use 4 layers of fyllo at a time. Cut into 5 x 5 inch squares. Place 2 heaping tablespoons of spinach filling across the top edge of the dough closest to you. Fold the two outside edges 1 inch towards the centre. Roll (jelly roll style) and place on greased baking sheet with the edge down. Brush over top with butter.

Bake for 25-30 minutes or until golden brown. Fyllo dough may be refrozen after thawing. Serve hot or cold. May also be served as an hors d'oeuvre.

VARIATION:
Substitute 1 pound ricotta cheese or cottage cheese for spinach to make cheese pastry. Omit salt, lemon juice and oil. Smaller or larger pastries may be made by cutting the fyllo to the size desired.

Spinach Pies

Fatayer bi Sabanikh   Meatless

1 **Savory Pie Dough recipe (page 134)**	½ **cup vegetable oil**
2 **large bunches of spinach**	1½ **tsp. salt**
(about 1 pound)	¼ **tsp. pepper**
1 **large onion (finely chopped)**	1 **cup pine nuts**
1 **cup parsley (finely chopped)**	**(optional)**
¾ **cup lemon juice**	**butter**

Prepare Savory Pie Dough.

Wash and drain spinach well. Chop small and place in large bowl. Add onions, parsley, lemon juice, oil, salt and pepper. Toss well. Set aside.

Place nuts in a dry frying pan on medium heat stirring constantly until golden brown. Add to spinach mixture.

Heat oven to 400°F.

Divide dough into 2 sections. Roll out to ⅛ inch thickness. Cut into 4 inch rounds. Place a heaping tablespoon of the mixture onto a round. Fold 3 sides of the dough over the spinach to form a triangle.

Make one at a time as the spinach will have a lot of juice. If necessary squeeze out some of the juice before placing in the dough.

Secure triangle by pressing on the edges of the dough as you fold (must be sealed well around the edges). A tiny opening may be left in the centre. If dough does not stick well in some places, put flour on finger tips to help seal. Place on greased cookie sheet. (Save the excess dough from the cuttings, roll into a ball, cover and let rest to use again).

Bake for 20-25 minutes or until golden brown.

Turn oven to broil for color, if necessary. Brush with butter.

Serve hot or cold.

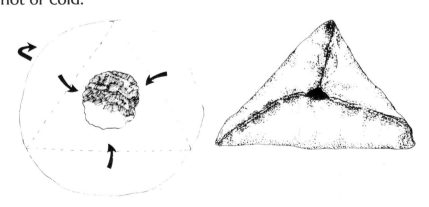

Savory Pie Dough

Ajeen Fatayer

2 cups warm water
2 Tbsp. sugar
1 package active dry yeast
¼ cup vegetable oil

2 tsp. salt
1 egg
5 cups flour

Place water and sugar in large bowl. Add yeast, stirring gently. Allow to rest for 5 minutes. Add oil, salt and egg. Fold in flour gradually.

Depending on the brand of the flour, use judgment to decide if more or less water is required. Knead until all flour leaves the edges of the bowl and dough is smooth.

Pat a little butter or oil over dough to prevent crusting. Cover with plastic sheet, then tea towel.

Let rest in a warm place for 30-40 minutes.

Use for Meat Pies (page 135), Spinach Pies (page 133), Potato Pies (page 134), Herb Bread (page 137), Talami (page 136) and Cheese Bread (page 137).

Potato Pies

Fatayer bi Batata

1 Savory Pie Dough recipe (page 134)
8 large potatoes (shredded)
¾ lb. ground beef
1 large onion (grated)

1½ tsp. salt
½ tsp. pepper
¼ tsp. cinnamon
soft butter

Prepare Savory Pie Dough and let rise.

Rinse shredded potatoes in cold water and squeeze out excess water. Place in large bowl. Add meat, onion, salt, pepper and cinnamon. Mix well.

Heat oven to 400°F.

Roll out half of the dough to ⅛ inch thickness on floured board. Cut into 3-4 inch rounds. (Save dough left from cutting. Roll and reuse).

Place a heaping tablespoon of the filling in a round. Bring up three edges to form a triangle. Secure edges of dough tightly leaving a ½ inch opening in the centre.

Place on greased cookie sheet and bake for approximately 20-25 minutes or until golden brown. Brush tops with butter.

Potato pies may be made larger or smaller by cutting the round to measurement desired.

Serve with fresh, cold yogurt, or stew dishes.

See illustration, page 133.

Meat Pies

Fatayer bi Laham

1 **Savory Pie Dough recipe (page 134)**	½ **tsp. pepper**
1½ **lbs. beef or lamb (ground)**	½ **tsp. cinnamon**
2 **large tomatoes (finely diced)**	1 **medium onion**
½ **cup parsley (finely chopped)**	**(finely chopped)**
¼ **cup tomato paste**	¼ **tsp. cayenne pepper**
½ **cup tomato sauce**	**soft butter**
2 **tsp. salt**	

Prepare one recipe of Savory Pie Dough. While dough is rising prepare filling.

Combine all remaining ingredients and mix well.

After dough rises, divide dough in half and roll to ⅛ inch thickness on a floured board. Cut with a round cutter 3 or 4 inches in diameter. (Save unused dough from cutting. Roll into a ball, cover, let rise to be used again).

Heat oven to 400°F.

Place a large tablespoon of the filling in each round within ½ inch of the edge. Bring the edges up and fold slightly towards the centre pressing the ½ inch edge down to make a ridge. Place on greased cookie sheet.

Bake for 15-20 minutes. If necessary, turn oven to broil until tops are golden brown. Brush edges with butter.

Serve with fresh, cold yogurt and salads. May be served with a squeeze of lemon juice on top. Excellent hot or cold.

Meat Filled Fyllo Pastry

Laham bi Ajeen Baklawa

1½ lbs. lean beef (ground)
2 Tbsp. butter
½ cup green onions (finely chopped)
¼ tsp. cayenne pepper (optional)
1½ tsp. salt

¼ tsp. pepper
¼ tsp. cinnamon
½ cup parsley (finely chopped)
1 lb. fyllo pastry dough
soft butter

If fyllo dough is frozen, thaw at room temperature for 4-5 hours.

Unroll and cover with damp cloth. Handle fyllo carefully while working with it. Always keep remaining dough covered with damp cloth.

Set oven at 350°F.

Place ground beef and butter in frying pan. Sauté until meat changes color. Do not fully cook. Add onions and seasonings and sauté for 1 minute. Stir in parsley. Remove from heat.

Use 4 layers of fyllo at a time and cut into 5 x 5 inch squares. Place 2 tablespoons of the filling across the top edge of the dough closest to you. Fold in the 2 outside edges 1 inch over the meat. Roll (jelly roll style) and place on greased baking sheet with the edge down. Brush butter over top of each roll.

Bake for 25-30 minutes or until golden brown.

Cool slightly and remove gently from baking sheet with a lifter.

Serve warm. May be served as hors d'oeuvres.

Talami

1 Savory Pie Dough recipe (page 134)

Divide dough into 6 rounds. Roll each out to ¼ inch in thickness, on floured board, cover with plastic sheet.

Let rest for 10-15 minutes.

Set oven at 450°F.

Place rounds on greased cookie sheets. Wet hand with water and press with finger tips several times. Bake for 8-10 minutes until lightly brown.

To serve: Tear pieces of Talami to eat with any food.

Cheese Bread

Talami bi Jibin   Meatless

1 recipe Savory Pie Dough (page 134)   **1 medium onion (grated fine)**
3 cheese patties preserved (page 127)   **¼ cup parsley**
¼ cup olive oil

Soak cheese patties in cold water for 2 hours.

Divide Savory Pie Dough into 6 rounds. Roll out to ¼ inch thickness on floured board. Cover with plastic sheet and leave to rise for 10-15 minutes.

While dough is rising, drain and mash the cheese with finger tips. Add olive oil, onions and parsley. Mix well.

Heat oven to 450°F.

Place rounds on a greased cookie sheet. Spread the cheese mixture evenly on top of the bread rounds. Press finger tips lightly several times into the cheese and dough.

Bake for 8-10 minutes. If necessary, turn oven to broil to lightly brown the top.

May be served with olives, fresh pepper cress and raw vegetables for a snack or breakfast.

Herb Bread

Manaiesh bi Zahtar   Meatless

Zahtar is a mixture of summer Savory, Thyme, Sumac and Sesame seeds. This may be purchased in Middle Eastern stores already prepared, ready to use.

1 Savory Pie Dough recipe (page 134)
¾ cup zahtar
1 ¼ cup vegetable or olive oil

Set oven at 450°F.

Divide dough into 6 rounds. Roll out each round to ¼ inch thickness on floured board. Cover with plastic sheet for 10-15 minutes.

Place rounds on greased baking sheet. Mix zahtar and oil together. Spread mixture evenly over the rounds, pressing finger tips into the dough several times.

Bake for approximately 8-10 minutes.

Serve for breakfast with olives, Arabic Cheese (page 127), or for a snack.

Pita Bread Fillings

In recent years Pita Bread has blended well with our western cuisine. This unique bread, when cut across the diameter, becomes a miraculous pocket. It serves as a pouch for hot or cold succulent foods, and the filling will not end up on your lap.

The wonderful pizza which has invaded our homes for years can now be prepared without a fuss. By using the whole Pita Bread as the base, add your favorite topping and presto, a pizza in minutes.

Fresh or toasted pieces of Pita Bread can be used for dipping into sauces and dips, and dropped into soups and tossed in salads.

Appetizers and Hor d'oeuvres are simplified when Pita Bread is on hand. To make pinwheel sandwiches, fill inside the Pita wedge or spread the filling over top of the wedges.

Throwing a party is no longer a chore. With lots of Pita Bread on hand, have your guests fill their own Pita pockets with various fillings you have prepared.

Take along Pita Bread when camping or hiking. It is so versatile, you will not have to worry about the condition it arrives in at the end of the road, it's flat like it's supposed to be.

A Lebanese meal without bread? Do not even think of it. In the Middle East, Bread is truly the staff of life. If a piece of bread accidently falls on the floor, it is picked up and kissed by the one who dropped it. The recipe for making Pita Bread can be found in the Savory Pastries and Bread section.

In Basket

Centre — *Shish Kabob and Pita*

Counterclockwise — *Tuna Pockets, Avocado Salad, Healthy Pockets, Fruit Pockets, Picnic Pockets, Salad in a Pita*

On Wooden Tray

Top — *Peanut Butter Banana Roll, Hamburger Pita Pockets, Frank in a Pita, Pita Pizza*

Shish Kabob and Pita

1 lb. lean beef or lamb (1 inch cubes)
2 Tbsp. olive oil
½ tsp. allspice
1 green pepper (cut into 1½ inch cubes)

12 fresh mushrooms
12 cherry tomatoes
salt and pepper to taste
Pita loaves (whole)

Place meat cubes in a bowl with olive oil and allspice. Mix well. Alternate meat and vegetables on skewers and place over hot charcoal to barbeque.

Serve, placing a skewer of the meat and vegetables across the whole Pita. Wrap the bread around the Shish Kabob and pull the skewer out leaving the meat and vegetables in the bread.

Serve with Hommous bi Tahini (page 21), Tabouli (page 43) or pickles.

Serves 4.

Tuna Pockets

2 cups flaked tuna
¼ cup celery (finely chopped)
2 green onions (finely chopped)

juice of half a lemon
shredded lettuce
2 Pita loaves (halved)

Combine tuna, celery, green onion and lemon juice in a mixing bowl. Open Pita pockets and fill with the mixture, adding shredded lettuce to each pocket.

Serves 4.

Avocado Salad Filling   Meatless

2 large, ripe avocados (peeled and sliced)
½ cup sliced radishes
½ cup diced celery
¼ cup chopped green onions
2 Tbsp. olive oil

2 Tbsp. lemon juice
¼ tsp. salt
¼ tsp. pepper
2 Pita loaves (halved)

Combine avocado, radishes, celery and green onions. In a cup mix oil, lemon juice, salt and pepper. Sprinkle over avocado mixture. Toss lightly. Open Pita pockets and fill.

Serves 4.

Healthy Pockets

Meatless

1 cup bean sprouts
1 cup alfalfa sprouts
½ cup cheddar cheese (grated)

salt and pepper to taste
juice of half a lemon
2 Pita loaves (halved)

Combine all above ingredients, except Pita, in mixing bowl. Fill Pita pockets with the mixture.

Serves 4.

Fruit Pockets

Meatless

A delightful snack.

2 cups fruit cocktail (drained)
½ cup watermelon (cubed)
½ cup papaya (cubed)
½ cup bananas (sliced)

¼ cup fresh yogurt or sour cream
shredded coconut (optional)
3 Pita loaves (halved)

Place all above ingredients, except Pita, in mixing bowl. Mix gently. Fill Pita pockets with mixture.

Serves 6.

Picnic Pockets

6 Romaine lettuce leaves
2 tomatoes (sliced)
1 green pepper (thinly sliced)
6 cold meat slices

6 cheese slices
salt and pepper to taste
3 Pita loaves (halved)

Fill Pita pockets with above ingredients. Sprinkle a dash of salt and pepper on filling.

Serves 6.

Salad in a Pita

2 cups lettuce (chopped)
½ cup cucumber (sliced)
1 tomato (cubed)
1 green pepper (sliced in rings)
½ cup bean sprouts

½ cup alfalfa sprouts
salt and pepper to taste
salad dressing (your choice)
2 Pita loaves (halved)

Combine all vegetables in salad bowl and toss. Open pita halves and fill with mixture. Add salt and pepper to taste and drizzle with salad dressing.

Serves 4.

Peanut Butter-Banana Pita Roll

2 bananas
peanut butter
honey
1 Pita loaf (whole)

Open Pita around the edges to make two rounds. Spread peanut butter and honey on each round. Peel banana and place in middle. Roll (jelly roll style) and serve.

Serves 2.

Hamburger Pita Pockets

4 hamburger patties
2 cheese slices (optional)
¼ cup shredded lettuce
1 dill pickle (sliced)
1 tomato (sliced)

ketchup
mustard
relish
1 Pita loaf (halved)

Fry, broil or barbeque hamburgers. Place 2 hamburger patties inside each Pita pocket with a slice of cheese. Add remaining toppings to taste.

Serves 2.

Frank in a Pita

A fun way to serve hot dogs.

4 large frankfurters	**ketchup**
mustard	onion (diced)
relish	**2 Pita loaves (whole)**

Cook franks (fry, bake, boil, broil or barbeque). Open the Pita around the edges to make 4 rounds. Place frank in the round, add desired topping and roll (jelly roll style).

Serves 4.

Pita Pizza

⅔ cup pizza sauce	**dash of salt and pepper**
ham, salami or pepperoni	**dash of oregano**
1 green pepper (thinly sliced)	**1 lb. mozzarella cheese**
3 tomatoes (thinly sliced)	**(shredded)**
½ cup mushrooms (thinly sliced)	**4 Pita loaves (whole)**

Preheat oven to 500°F. Use the whole Pita. Spread on the pizza sauce then add slices of meat to cover the Pita. Arrange the peppers, tomatoes and mushrooms over top, or use your own topping. Sprinkle with oregano, salt and pepper. Spread shredded cheese evenly over top. Bake for 8-10 minutes.

Serves 4.

Hors D'Oeuvres

Pita Bread may be filled with any preferred filling.
(1) Cut pita in half. Fill inside of pockets and cut in half again.
(2) Cut Pita loaf into wedges. Fill individual wedges.
(3) Cut Pita into wedges and add your favorite topping, being creative in garnishing.
(4) Open Pita around the edges to make 2 rounds. Spread each with filling. Roll jelly roll style. Cut diagonally and insert a toothpick to hold together.

Pita Chips

3 Pita (whole)
½ cup butter or oil
2 cloves garlic (crushed) *or*
1 tsp. garlic powder

oregano
thyme

Open Pita Bread around the edges to make 6 rounds. Mix oil and garlic together and brush on each side of the Pita Bread. Cut each round into eight wedges. Sprinkle with oregano and thyme. Toss well. Place wedges on a baking sheet. Spread out on the baking sheet and bake at 350°F for 10-15 minutes or until crisp.

Roast Beef Pockets

8 slices of cold roast beef
  dill pickles (sliced)
  mustard

tomatoes (sliced)
shredded lettuce
4 Pita loaves (halved)

Open Pita pockets and spread mustard inside. Fill each pocket with 2 slices of meat. Add pickles, tomatoes and shredded lettuce.

Serves 8.

Cheese Crisps

2 Pita loaves (whole)
6 slices of cheese
  thyme

Split Pita Bread around the edges leaving 3 or 4 inches intact. Place 3 cheese slices inside. Sprinkle a little thyme over the cheese. Replace top layer of Pita, covering the cheese. Place in 400°F oven for 4-5 minutes.

VARIATION:
Add thinly sliced tomatoes, or sliced Spanish onion to the cheese.

Avocado Clam Dip

1 clove garlic
¼ tsp. salt
2 large, ripe avocados (pitted)
½ cup canned whole clams
   (well drained and finely chopped)

2 Tbsp. mild green chilies
   (finely chopped)
1 Tbsp. lemon juice
1 Tbsp. grated onion
   dash of cayenne
   Pita Bread

Crush garlic clove and salt in a mixing bowl. Add avocado and mash to a smooth texture with a fork or force through a sieve.

Add clams, green chilies, lemon juice, onion and cayenne. Mix well. Cover and chill.

To serve: Tear off pieces of Pita Bread and dip into the mixture. Pita Bread can also be cut into wedges and placed on baking sheet in a 400 °F oven for 4-5 minutes, or until crisp.

Liver and Onion Filling

1 lb. liver (cut into thin strips)
½ tsp. salt
¼ tsp. pepper
2 Tbsp. vegetable oil

1 large onion (thinly sliced)
1 cup fresh mushrooms (sliced)
¼ cup green peppers (chopped)
3 Pita loaves (halved)

Season the liver. Heat oil in skillet. Add liver and onion. Sauté for 3 minutes. Add mushrooms and green peppers. Sauté for 2 more minutes. Fill Pita pockets with the mixture.

Serves 6.

Meatloaf Pockets

2 lbs. ground beef
1 Pita loaf
1 small onion (grated)
1 egg
1 tsp. salt

¼ tsp. pepper
3 Pita loaves (halved)
   cucumber (sliced)
   pickles (sliced)
   mustard

Preheat oven to 350 °F. Crisp Pita loaf by placing in oven to dry. Roll with rolling pin to make crumbs. In a mixing bowl place beef, Pita crumbs, onion, egg, salt and pepper. Shape into a loaf and bake for 60 minutes. Cool, slice and fill inside of Pita pockets. Add cucumber, pickles and mustard.

Serves 6.

Lobster-Avocado Salad

2 avocados (peeled and diced)
1½ cups cooked lobster (diced)
3 Tbsp. lemon juice
¾ cup celery (diced)

3 Tbsp. olive oil
¼ tsp. salt
¼ tsp. pepper
2 Pita loaves (halved)

Combine first seven ingredients in mixing bowl. Chill. Use as filling inside Pita pockets.

Serves 4.

Fishy Pockets

1 lb. fish fillets (breaded)
½ Taratour recipe (page 26)
2 Pita loaves (halved)

Broil the fish on a greased cookie sheet for approximately 5 minutes on each side. Fill Pita pockets with fish and spoon on Taratour Sauce.

Serves 4.

Avocado-Cheese Filling   Meatless

2 ripe avocados (peeled and sliced)
2 Tbsp. lemon juice
2 cups Monterey Jack cheese (grated)
2 cups alfalfa sprouts

3 Tbsp. Yogurt Spread
(page 124)
salt and pepper to taste
2 Pita loaves (halved)

Place avocado in mixing bowl and sprinkle with lemon juice. Add cheese and sprouts. Toss lightly. Open pockets and spread Yogurt Spread inside. Add filling and season with salt and pepper.

Serves 4.

Beef Stroganoff Pita Filling

¼ cup flour
1½ tsp. salt
¼ tsp. pepper
2 lbs. beef tenderloin
(cut into very thin strips)
¼ cup butter
1 clove garlic (crushed)
1 cup onions (coarsely chopped)

1 lb. mushrooms (sliced)
2 Tbsp. butter (soft)
3 Tbsp. flour
2 cups beef broth
2 Tbsp. tomato paste
1 cup sour cream
4 Pita loaves (halved)

Coat beef with mixture of flour, salt and pepper. Brown meat in butter in skillet. Add garlic, onion and mushrooms. Sauté until onion is lightly browned. Set aside.

In a small bowl, blend 2 tablespoons of softened butter and 3 tablespoons flour. Add broth and tomato paste. Stir until well blended. Add this to the meat and vegetable mixture.

Mix well, return to heat and cook until thickened. Add sour cream and heat thoroughly on moderate heat.

Open Pita pockets and fill with the mixture.

Serves 8.

Meatball Stew in Pockets

3 Tbsp. vegetable oil
1 green pepper (sliced)
1 small onion (sliced)
1 cup celery (diced)
2 cups tomato sauce
1 lb. ground beef

1 medium onion (grated)
1 Pita loaf
1 egg
1 tsp. salt
¼ tsp. pepper
3 Pita loaves (halved)

Prepare Pita crumbs by placing whole Pita loaf in 350°F oven until dry. Roll with rolling pin to make crumbs.

In saucepan place oil, green pepper, sliced onion and celery. Sauté for 2 minutes. Add tomato sauce and simmer for 10 minutes.

Meanwhile, prepare meatballs. In a mixing bowl, place beef, grated onion, Pita crumbs, egg, salt and pepper. Mix well.

Shape into small balls and broil until slightly browned. Add meatballs and drippings to the vegetables and sauce. Simmer for 30 minutes.

Serve inside Pita pockets with meatballs and sauce.

Serves 6.

Chicken Livers in Pockets

A delicious way to serve liver.

1 lb. chicken livers	dash of cayenne pepper
3 Tbsp. butter (melted)	2 Tbsp. prepared mustard
⅔ cup flour	1 clove garlic (crushed)
2 tsp. butter	2 tsp. Worcestershire sauce
1 tsp. minced onion	2 Pita loaves (halved)

Dip liver in melted butter and coat with flour. Broil for 4 minutes on each side. Melt 2 teaspoons butter in frying pan. Stir in onions, cayenne, mustard, garlic and Worcestershire sauce. Sauté until onions are transparent. Fill pockets with broiled liver and spoon onion mixture over. Serve at once.

Serves 4.

Chicken-Mushroom Pockets

A creamy, hot chicken filling.

3 Tbsp. butter	½ tsp. salt
1 cup fresh mushrooms (sliced)	¼ tsp. pepper
¼ cup flour	1½ cups cooked chicken (diced)
1½ cups milk	2 Pita loaves (halved)

Melt butter in skillet. Add mushrooms and sauté until tender. Stir in flour. Add milk and seasonings gradually, stirring until sauce is smooth and thickened. Add chicken. Simmer for 5 minutes, stirring occasionally. Serve inside Pita pockets at once.

Serves 4.

Hash Pockets

¼ cup minced onion
1 Tbsp. minced celery
1 Tbsp. minced green pepper
¼ tsp. minced garlic
1 Tbsp. butter

2 cups boiled potatoes (diced)
1½ cups left-over meat (diced)
    salt and pepper to taste
2 Pita loaves (halved)

Sauté onion, celery, green pepper and garlic in butter. Add diced potatoes, meat, salt and pepper. Cook until heated throughout. Open pockets and fill with the mixture.

Serve with fresh, cold yogurt.

Serves 4.

Taco Pockets

1 lb. ground beef
1 clove garlic (crushed)
1 medium onion (finely chopped)
1 cup tomato sauce
1 Tbsp. Worcestershire sauce
1 tsp. chili powder
¼ tsp. Tabasco sauce

1 tsp. cumin
5 Pita loaves (halved)
    shredded lettuce
    cheddar cheese (grated)
    Spanish onion (chopped)
    tomatoes (chopped)
    Taco sauce

Brown beef in skillet, breaking up the meat with a fork. Drain fat. Add garlic, onion, tomato sauce, Worcestershire sauce, chili powder, Tabasco sauce and cumin. Stir well and simmer for 25 minutes. Spoon beef mixture into the pockets. Top with lettuce, cheese, onions, tomatoes and Taco sauce.

Serves 10.

Tabouli Pockets   Meatless

1 Tabouli recipe (page 43)
6 Romaine lettuce leaves (chopped)
3 Pita loaves (halved)

Open Pita halves. Line with lettuce leaves. Fill with the Tabouli.

Serves 6.

Salmon Dainties

3 Pita loaves
¼ cup butter
1 clove garlic (crushed)
2 cups flaked salmon

¼ cup dill pickle (chopped)
¼ cup sour cream
¼ tsp. salt
¼ tsp. pepper

Open the Pita around the edges to make 6 rounds. Combine butter and garlic and spread on each round. Combine the rest of the ingredients. Divide the mixture evenly among the 6 Pita rounds. Spread the mixture to reach the edges. Roll jelly roll style. Slice into ½ inch pieces. Insert a toothpick to hold together.

Serves 3-4.

Curried Turkey Pockets

¼ cup butter
¼ cup slivered almonds
2 tsp. curry powder
¼ cup onions (chopped)
2 Tbsp. flour
1 tsp. salt

¼ tsp. pepper
1 cup turkey or chicken broth
2 cups cooked turkey (diced)
1 tsp. grated lemon peel
1 tsp. grated orange peel
3 Pita loaves (halved)

Melt butter in skillet. Add almonds and sauté until almonds are lightly browned. Add curry powder. Stir in onions and cook until tender. Blend in flour and seasonings. Add broth, cook and stir until boiling. Reduce heat and simmer for 2 minutes. Add turkey, lemon and orange peel. Cook for 3 minutes. Spoon into pockets and serve at once.

Serves 6.

Turkey-Tomato Pockets

1 medium onion (chopped)
1 Tbsp. butter
¾ cup tomato ketchup
1 tsp. mustard
½ cup chopped celery
¼ cup water
¼ cup lemon juice

1 Tbsp. Worcestershire sauce
2 Tbsp. brown sugar
¼ tsp. pepper
¼ tsp. cayenne pepper
4 thick slices of cooked turkey
2 Pita loaves (halved)

In skillet, sauté onions in butter until transparent. Add all remaining ingredients, except turkey and Pita, and simmer (covered) for 15 minutes. Add turkey slices to sauce. Cover and simmer for another 10 minutes. Place one turkey slice and some sauce inside each pocket. Serve at once.

Serves 4.

Sloppy Joe Pita Pockets

1 Tbsp. vegetable oil
½ cup onion (chopped)
½ cup green pepper (chopped)
1 ½ lbs. ground beef

2 cups tomato sauce
2 Tbsp. chili sauce
2 tsp. Worcestershire sauce
3 Pita loaves (halved)

Heat oil in skillet. Add onion, green pepper and ground beef, breaking up the beef with a fork. Cook until meat is browned. Drain fat. Add the three sauces. Stir for 1 minute. Open pockets and spoon in the filling.

Serves 6.

Chicken Pita Pockets

2 cups cooked chicken (diced)
1 tomato (diced)
2 green onions (chopped)
½ cup celery (chopped)
¼ cup dill pickles (diced)

1 cup Yogurt Spread (page 124)
salt and pepper to taste
shredded lettuce
3 Pita loaves (halved)

In mixing bowl combine the first seven ingredients. Toss well. Fill inside of pockets with the mixture, adding shredded lettuce to each.

Serves 6.

Oyster Loaf Pockets

2 whole Pita
1 lb. fresh oysters (chopped)
3 eggs (beaten)
½ cup evaporated milk
½ tsp. salt
¼ tsp. pepper
1 tsp. Italian dressing
1 Tbsp. butter

2 green onions (finely chopped)
1 green pepper (finely chopped)
¼ cup celery (finely chopped)
¼ cup parsley (finely chopped)
3 Pita loaves (halved)
  lemon wedges
  chili sauce

Heat oven to 375°F. Place 2 whole Pita in oven until dry. Roll with rolling pin to make crumbs.

Combine crumbs with oysters and mix thoroughly. Add eggs, milk, salt, pepper and Italian dressing.

Melt butter in skillet. Add onions and green pepper and sauté. Add oyster mixture, celery and parsley. Mix well. Turn mixture into a greased loaf pan.

Bake for 30 minutes.

Cool and slice into 6 portions. Place a slice of oyster loaf in each Pita half. Squeeze lemon over filling and spread with chili sauce.

Serves 6.

Tuna Patties in Pita

1 whole Pita loaf
1 cup tuna
½ cup minced onion
¼ tsp. salt
¼ tsp. pepper
3 Tbsp. celery (diced)

2 Tbsp. parsley (finely chopped)
½ tsp. tarragon
1 egg (beaten)
¼ cup butter
1 Pita loaf (halved)
  lemon juice

To make Pita crumbs place 1 whole Pita in oven until dry. Roll with rolling pin to make crumbs.

Combine tuna, onion, salt, pepper, celery, parsley, tarragon, egg and Pita crumbs in a mixing bowl. Mix well. Form into 4 patties. Melt butter in skillet. Brown patties. Place 2 patties in each pocket. Add a squeeze of lemon to each.

Serves 2.

Pita Burritos

Nellie's Special

1 cup ground beef	4 Pita Bread (whole)
2 Tbsp. vegetable oil	cheddar cheese (grated)
1 cup refried beans	shredded lettuce
1 tsp. salt	diced tomatoes
¼ tsp. pepper	hot Taco sauce

Place ground meat and oil in a skillet. Cook on low heat, breaking up the meat with a fork until meat is brown.

Add the refried beans, salt and pepper. Continue cooking until beans are hot.

Spread several tablespoons of the filling on top of the Pita. Add remaining ingredients to taste. Roll jelly roll style.

Serves 4.

Fried Vegetable Pita Pockets　　　　Meatless

3 Tbsp. vegetable oil	1 cup bean sprouts
1 stalk celery (diced)	salt and pepper to taste
1 zucchini (thinly sliced)	½ tsp. oregano
1 green pepper (thinly sliced)	2 Pita Bread (cut in half)

Place oil in skillet with celery. Stir and fry on high heat for 1 minute. Add zucchini, green peppers and bean sprouts. Lower heat to medium, fry vegetables until limp but crisp. Add seasonings. Fill Pita Pockets with the mixture.

Serves 4.

Pita Breakfast

4 strips of bacon	1 Pita Bread (cut in half)
4 eggs	1 tomato (thinly sliced)
salt and pepper to taste	

Cut bacon strips into 1 inch pieces. Place in skillet over medium heat. Cook until crisp.

Drain all fat except 1 tablespoon. Break eggs over the bacon pieces and add salt and pepper to taste. Stir gently until eggs are set.

Open Pita half to form a pocket. Place half of the bacon and egg mixture into each pocket. Add sliced tomatoes.

Serves 2.

VARIATION:
Substitute sausages for the bacon. Proceed with above directions.

Beef Filling

1 lb. steak (very thinly sliced)
1 onion (thinly sliced)
1 clove garlic (crushed)
½ tsp. basil
½ tsp. salt
¼ tsp. pepper
4 Tbsp. butter
1 cup red cabbage (sliced)
2 Pita loaves (halved)

Combine steak with onion, garlic and seasonings in a skillet. Add butter and sauté for 5 minutes. Add cabbage and sauté for about another 10 minutes, until cabbage is tender. Open pockets and spoon in the filling. Serve at once.

Serves 4.

Chicken-Pineapple Pita Pockets

2 cups cooked chicken (cubed)
1 cup pineapple chunks
½ cup mayonnaise
½ cup celery (diced)
½ cup cashew nuts (chopped)
½ tsp. salt
¼ tsp. pepper
2 Pita loaves (halved)

Combine all above ingredients, except Pita, in a mixing bowl. Toss well and chill. When ready to serve, fill pockets.

Serves 4.

Chicken-Fruit Filling

3 cups cooked chicken (diced)
1 cup celery (finely chopped)
1 cup canned mandarin oranges (drained)
1 cup pineapple tidbits (drained)
½ cup slivered almonds (roasted)
½ cup sour cream
¼ tsp. salt
½ tsp. marjoram
3 Pita loaves (halved)

Combine all above ingredients, except Pita, in a mixing bowl. Chill. Fill pockets with the mixture just before serving.

Serves 6.

Sweets and Beverages

There is an abundance of fresh fruit in Lebanon. Fruit is usually offered to visitors and is also served after a meal. In contrast to western tradition, pastries or sweets are not necessarily served after a meal as dessert, but with Arabic coffee late in the evening.

Some of the pastries in this section are traditionally prepared for religious occasions or festivities. Today the homemaker uses the recipes year-round.

Baklava is the most popular Lebanese sweet. It is soaked in honey syrup and butter and filled with nuts. It is a succulent, tantalizing dessert.

Beverages, of course, include the famed Arabic coffee, served in small demitasse cups. Sweetened coffee is served on any occasion and bitter coffee is appropriately offered on sad occasions.

Yogurt mixed with water is a refreshing drink, particularly if fresh fruit is blended with it to vary the flavour.

Top — *Arabic Coffee*

Centre — *Baklava*

Counterclockwise — *Deep Fried Rossettes, Awwami, Kaak, Wheatlet Squares, Ma'amoul with Wheatlets*

Baklava

Baklawa

The Queen of Lebanese pastries. Famous throughout the world.

2 cups walnuts or pistachio nuts (finely chopped)	**1 lb. package fyllo dough**
½ cup sugar	**1 lb. unsalted butter**
	2 Syrup recipes (pages 160)

If fyllo is frozen defrost at room temperature 4-5 hours.

When working with fyllo dough always keep sheets, that are not being used, covered with a damp cloth.

Combine nuts and sugar, mixing well. Set aside.

Butter the bottom of a 14 x 10 inch baking pan.

Divide the package of fyllo dough into two sections; leaving one half for the bottom layer and the other half for the top.

Melt the butter.

Lay 2 sheets of fyllo over the bottom of the pan. Brush on butter then take two more sheets and lay them over the two sheets in the pan. Repeat this procedure until half of the pound is used. Spoon the nuts evenly over the last layer.

Continue to butter two sheets and place them over the nuts, repeating the same procedure until all sheets are used. Brush the top layer with butter. Cut into 1½ inch diamond shaped pieces.

Bake at 300°F for 1 hour or until golden brown. Remove from oven and pour cold syrup over the Baklava. Saturate well.

VARIATION:
For a different Baklava shape take 2 fyllo sheets and brush lightly with melted butter. Place 3-4 tablespoons of the filling along the wide edge of the fyllo. Roll as in jelly roll. Brush butter along the top. Cut diagonally into 2 inch lengths. Place on buttered 10 x 14 inch pan closely side by side. Continue until fyllo and nut filling is used. Bake at 300°F for 45 minutes or until golden brown. Remove from oven. Spoon cold syrup over each piece, saturating well. Repeat 2 times over each piece until all syrup is used.

Syrup

Atter

2 cups sugar, or honey	**1 geranium leaf or ½ tsp. rose**
1 cup water	**water (optional)**
1 Tbsp. lemon juice	

If honey is substituted for sugar use only ½ cup water in the recipe, following these directions.

Combine sugar and water. Stir until dissolved. Boil over medium heat for 5 minutes.

Add lemon juice (and geranium leaf or rose water if desired). Boil for 5 more minutes. Remove from heat and cool.

Deep Fried Rossettes

Mshabbak

A soft plastic bottle with a small hole in the tip is used. A ketchup or mustard bottle may be used, but a clean dish detergent bottle is also suitable. Syrup may be divided into 2 or 3 parts and desired food coloring may be added to each.

3 cups warm water	**½ cup cornstarch**
1 tsp. sugar	**oil for deep frying**
1½ tsp. yeast	**2 Syrup recipes (page 160)**
2¼ cups flour	**food colouring**
sprinkle of salt	

Make Syrup and set aside.

Place water in large mixing bowl. Stir in sugar and dissolve. Add yeast and leave to rise for 5 minutes.

Using an egg beater on low speed, gradually beat in flour, salt, and cornstarch. Beat until smooth (approximately 3 minutes). Cover and leave to rise for 30-40 minutes. This recipe will be runny.

Fill plastic bottle with batter.

Heat oil in heavy skillet for deep frying. Squeeze batter into oil, forming a round ring 2-3 inches in diameter, and filling the inside of the ring with the batter, forming a lacey rossette.

4-5 rossettes may be made at a time. Fry until golden brown turning once. Remove from oil with a slotted spoon and drop into cool syrup. Remove and place on platter.

VARIATION:
Food coloring is not necessary. After frying rossettes, drop into cold syrup.

Kaak

1 tsp. sugar	1½ cups milk (warm)
½ cup water	5 eggs
2 tsp. yeast	¼ cup melted butter
6½ cups flour	1 cup milk
1½ cups sugar	½ cup sugar
1 tsp. baking powder	

Dissolve sugar in ½ cup water, add yeast and set aside for 5 minutes.

In a large mixing bowl, place flour, sugar and baking powder. Make a well in the centre of the flour mixture. Place 1½ cups warm milk, eggs, butter and yeast mixture inside the well. Knead until flour leaves the sides of the bowl and dough is smooth. Cover with plastic sheet, then a tea towel. Leave in a warm place to rise for 30-40 minutes.

Knead again, cover and leave to rise for 30 minutes further.

Heat oven to 400°F.

Cut a piece of dough the size of a walnut. Roll into a rope shape approximately 5-6 inches long, join ends together to form a ring, press ends together to secure.

Place on a greased cookie sheet. Bake for 10-15 minutes to a golden brown.

Meanwhile prepare glaze. Place 1 cup of milk in a saucepan, add sugar. Place over medium heat, stir to dissolve sugar. Remove from heat.

Dip warm Kaak in the milk and sugar glaze, place on tray to dry.

Serve with coffee, tea or as a snack.

VARIATION:
Sesame seeds may be used for topping on the Kaak. Beat 1 egg white, brush over the Kaak after the ring has been formed. Spread sesame seeds on a plate. Place the egg brushed side over the sesame seeds, press lightly. Place on greased baking sheet with the sesame side up. Bake as above.

Wheatlet Squares

Nammura (Hrisi)

Make the syrup first. Then make the squares.

SYRUP FOR SQUARES

  3 cups sugar
1 ½ cups water
1 ½ Tbsp. lemon juice

Combine all above ingredients together in saucepan. Stir to dissolve sugar. Bring to boil over medium heat. Turn to low heat, simmer for 10 minutes. Set aside to cool.

NOTE: ¾ cup of the syrup will be used in the mixture for the squares. Save the remainder of the syrup to be used for squares after they are baked.

SQUARES

  Sesame Seed Paste or butter
  (for greasing pan)
2 cups wheatlets or Cream of Wheat
½ cup soft butter
1 cup yogurt (plain)

1 ¼ tsp. baking powder
  blanched almonds
¾ cup Syrup from
  above recipe

Heat oven to 350 °F.

For thick squares grease an 8 x 8 inch pan with Sesame Seed paste or butter. Grease a 9 x 12 inch pan if thin squares are preferred.

Combine remaining ingredients except blanched almonds. Mix well, do not beat. Pour mixture into pan, spreading batter evenly. Shake and lightly drop pan to settle mixture.

Lightly press a knife blade into the mixture (do not cut through) and mark 1 ½ inch squares or diamond shapes. Place 1 almond in the centre of each square. Bake in oven for 35-40 minutes. Remove and cut square through. Turn oven to 375 °F. Return to oven and bake for another 25-30 minutes or until golden brown.

Remove from oven and pour remainder of cold syrup over the squares.

VARIATION:
Add ½ cup shredded coconut to wheatlet mixture.

Ma'amoul with Wheatlets

Ma'amoul bi Smeedi

6 cups wheatlets
2 cups unsalted butter (melted)
1 tsp. sugar
1 cup water or milk (lukewarm)

½ tsp. yeast
icing sugar

FILLING

2 cups walnuts (finely chopped)
½ cup sugar

Place wheatlets in a large bowl, add butter and mix, rubbing well with hands. Cover and set aside for 6-8 hours.

Combine filling and set aside.

Dissolve the sugar in the water or milk, add the yeast, stir slightly, and set aside for 5 minutes. Add this to be the wheatlet mixture, mixing well. If required add a little more water to make dough pliable.

Form a small ball the size of a walnut and make a cavity in the centre. Place a teaspoonful of the nut filling inside and close, sealing well. Shape the top like a dome. Decorate with the tines of a fork. Place on an ungreased baking sheet, with the dome shape up, and the flat surface on the sheet.

Bake in 300°F oven for 30-40 minutes. Color should be a very light brown. Cool thoroughly. Sprinkle icing sugar over top.

Always store Ma'amoul in an air tight container (they freeze well). Do not sprinkle icing sugar on top until just before serving.

NOTE: A special decorative wooden mold may be used, it is called a "Tabih". To use, place a little oil or flour in the mold, then place the walnut sized dough inside. Make a cavity in the centre, place filling inside and close, sealing well. Turn the mold upside down; with one hand underneath give the top edge of the mold a tap on the counter top or table, the ma'amoul will fall out. Place on a baking sheet with the flat side down and the dome shape up.

Awwami

1 package dry yeast	½ tsp. salt
½ cup warm water	1½ cups warm water
1 tsp. sugar	oil, as required for deep frying
3 cups flour	2 Syrup recipes (page 160)

Dissolve dry yeast in ½ cup warm water and sugar. Set aside for 5-10 minutes.

Place flour and salt in bowl. Gradually add yeast mixture and 1½ cups warm water. Mix well. This will be a soft dough.

Let rise in warm place until double in bulk (2-3 hours). Drop by teaspoonful into hot deep frying oil and fry until golden brown.

Remove with slotted spoon and dip immediately into cold syrup (Atter).

Place on platter to serve.

Shortbread

Ghoraibi

1 cup unsalted butter (soft)
1 cup sugar – berry or icing sugar
2 cups flour

Beat butter and sugar until light for approximately 2-3 minutes.

Gradually mix in flour (with hand). Mix well. Mixture should be pliable when shaped into a ball. If required, add 1 or 2 tablespoons of flour.

Heat oven to 300 °F.

Take a small amount of the mixture and shape into a ball the size of a walnut. Flatten slightly and made a small indentation in the centre with finger. Place on an ungreased cookie sheet and bake for 20-25 minutes.

VARIATION:
(1) Shapes can vary. Roll out on a slightly floured board and cut with a cookie cutter.
(2) Shape each one into a crescent, a diamond, or "S" shape.
(3) Using the round shape, make a depression in centre and fill with ¼ teaspoon of crushed walnuts or pistachios. Close, pat down lightly and bake.

Ma'amoul with Flour

Ma'amoul bi Tahein

2 cups unsalted butter (soft)
½ cup berry sugar
6 cups flour
    milk (lukewarm)

Nut filling from Ma'amoul
with Wheatlets (page 163) or
Date filling from Ma'amoul
with Dates (page 165)

Place butter, sugar and flour in a mixing bowl. Rub together with hands until well mixed. Gradually mix in warm milk starting with 1 cup and adding more as required. Dough should be a little softer than pie dough. There is no need to leave to rest.

Pinch off a little of the dough. Make a cavity in the centre, place filling inside and close. Form a dome shape whether by hand or with the special "Tabih" used in the other 2 Ma'amoul recipes. Follow the same directions using either the nut filling or the date filling.

Ma'amoul with Date Filling

Ma'amoul bi Ajwi

This recipe uses date filling. Follow the directions for Ma'amoul with Wheatlets, using this filling recipe.

1 recipe Ma'amoul with Wheatlets
    (page 163)
¼ cup butter
1 lb. dates (chopped)

½ cup walnuts (finely chopped)
    (optional)
¼ tsp. nutmeg

Melt butter in heavy saucepan on low heat. Add dates and stir, breaking up the date pieces. Cook, stirring occasionally, until mixture is soft. Add nuts if desired and nutmeg; stir and remove from heat. Cool. Place a teaspoon of the filling inside the cavity, close and continue using the recipe for Ma'amoul with Wheatlets.

Sesame Crisps

Barazik

Helly's Special

A delicious crispy cookie.

1 lb. unsalted butter (soft)	1 egg white (slightly beaten)
2 cups sugar	3 Tbsp. sugar
4 ¼ cups flour	2 cups sesame seeds

Beat with electric beater (on low speed) ½ pound of the butter and 1 cup sugar. Gradually beat in remaining butter and sugar until mixture is light (approximately 3-4 minutes). Gradually fold in flour. Knead well. Mixture should be a little sticky. Set aside.

Set oven at 400°F.

Mix egg whites, sugar and sesame seeds together in a small mixing bowl. Mixture will be dry. Place 2 heaping tablespoons of the sesame mixture in the centre of a plate.

Take a small amount of the flour mixture, roll into a ball the size of a walnut and place over sesame seeds. Press down lightly on the pattie to flatten it to a thin round approximately 3-4 inches in diameter, keeping the edges together while pressing. Lift, using an egg lifter, and place on an ungreased cookie sheet, sesame side up.

Bake for 10-15 minutes or until golden brown. Cool before removing from cookie sheet.

Fried Dough
Zlaby

1 tsp. sugar	2½ cups flour
1¼ cup lukewarm water	oil (for frying)
1 tsp. yeast	sugar – granulated, icing or berry
1 Tbsp. vegetable oil	(to sprinkle on top)
½ tsp. salt	

In a large bowl, dissolve sugar in water. Add yeast. Leave aside for 5 minutes.

Add the 1 tablespoon oil and salt to the yeast mixture. Gradually fold in the flour. Knead to a smooth texture. Smooth a few drops of oil over the dough. Cover with a plastic sheet, then a tea towel and leave in a warm place to rise for 40-45 minutes.

Roll out dough on lightly floured board to ½ inch in thickness. Cut into 3 x 5 inch strips.

Heat oil for frying. Fry strips on both sides to a light golden color. Remove from oil and drain on absorbent towels.

Sprinkle with sugar on one side only, while still warm.

May be served warm or cold.

VARIATION:
4 or 5 inch rounds may also be made; pinch the edges and fry.

Sesame Honey Squares
Soomsoom mah Assal

1 cup honey	½ cup walnuts or almonds (chopped)
½ tsp. lemon	1 tsp. Sesame Seed Paste (Tahini)
1 cup sesame seeds (roasted)	for greasing pan

Place honey in saucepan and bring to a boil over medium heat. Add lemon. Turn heat to low and boil for 1 minute.

Add roasted sesame seeds and chopped nuts. Bring to boil again for 1 minute.

Remove from heat. Spread sesame seed paste in the bottom of an 8 x 8 inch pan. Pour honey mixture in. Cool, then cut into squares. Keep refrigerated.

NOTE: To roast sesame seeds, place in a dry frying pan over low heat, stirring constantly until seeds are a light brown.

VARIATION:
Shredded coconut or granola may be substituted for the nuts.

Crescents
Sambusik

FILLING
   2 cups walnuts (finely chopped)
   ½ cup sugar

PASTRY
1½ cups unsalted butter (soft)
   5 cups flour
   ¼ cup sugar

1 tsp. baking powder
   water (lukewarm)
2 Syrup recipes (page 160)

In a small bowl combine the walnuts and sugar; mix and set aside.

Mix butter and flour together, rubbing with hands. Mix in sugar and baking powder. Add enough water to make the mixture the consistency of pie dough.

Flour the countertop and roll out dough with a rolling pin to ⅛ inch thickness. Cut with a cookie cutter into 2 inch rounds. Place a teaspoon of the filling inside each round. Bring one end over to shape a half moon or crescent. Pinch edges well to secure. Place on ungreased cookie sheet.

Set oven at 350°F. Bake for 15-20 minutes to a light golden brown. Remove from cookie sheet and dip into the cold syrup while crescents are still hot. Remove from syrup with a slotted spoon.

Cheese Filled Squares
Knafi bi Jibin

   2 lbs. Ricotta cheese
   1 cup sugar
   1 lb. shredded pastry (Knafi dough)

¾ cup melted butter (unsalted)
1 Syrup recipe (page 160)

Set oven at 325°F.

Combine the Ricotta cheese and sugar. Mix with a fork. Set aside.

Place the shredded pastry in a large mixing bowl. Drizzle butter over top. Mix with hands gently coating the pastry with the butter.

Spread half of the shredded pastry evenly on the bottom of a 9x13 inch pan, pressing down with hands. Add the cheese mixture spreading evenly. Place the remainder of the shredded pastry evenly over top. Bake for 1 hour or until golden brown. Remove from oven and pour cold syrup over top.

Serve hot for better results, but may be served cold.

Rice Flour Squares

Knafi bi Ruz

Renée's Special

Gum Arabic is obtained from Acacia trees and is used in sweets. It may be found in Middle Eastern retail stores and specialty sections in some supermarkets.

6 cups milk, cream or half and half	**1 tsp. rosewater**
1½ cups rice flour	**1 tsp. ground Gum Arabic (miski)**
1½ cups sugar	**¾ cup crumbs (wafer or biscuit)**
1 tsp. vanilla	**¼ cup melted butter (unsalted)**
1 tsp. almond extract	**1 Syrup recipe (page 160)**

Butter a 9x13 inch baking pan.

Place milk or cream in a heavy saucepan. Add rice flour, sugar, vanilla, almond extract and rosewater. Stir constantly over medium heat for 5 minutes. Turn heat to low and add Gum Arabic, stirring for 4-5 minutes or until mixture begins to bubble. Remove from heat and pour mixture into the baking pan spreading evenly.

Sprinkle crumbs evenly to cover top. Spoon melted butter along the edges between the mixture and the pan.

Set oven at 500°F. Place in oven for 10 minutes. Remove, cool and refrigerate. Cut into 2 inch squares.

Serve cold with 2 tablespoons of cold syrup over each serving.

VARIATION:
Replace the rice flour with cream of wheat. Proceed with above recipe.

Filled Suzettes

Atayif

BATTER
 ½ tsp. dry yeast
 1 tsp. sugar
1 ¼ cups lukewarm water
1 ½ cups flour

FILLING
 2 cups walnuts (finely chopped)
 1 Tbsp. sugar
 2 Syrup recipes (page 160)

Dissolve the yeast and sugar together in the water in a mixing bowl. Let stand for approximately 10 minutes.

Gradually add flour, stirring to smooth batter. Cover and set aside for 1 hour.

Combine the walnuts and sugar together in a mixing bowl. Set aside.

Place a heavy skillet on medium heat. Wipe the bottom with a paper towel dipped in oil. Place 3 tablespoons of the batter in the pan, tilt a little to make batter even into approximately 3 inch rounds (as for crepes). Cook only one side but make sure the top is dry.

Remove from pan onto a baking sheet. Immediately place a teaspoon of walnut mixture in the centre of the round. Bring one side over to cover the nuts. The shape will resemble a half moon. Press the edges tightly to secure. Continue this with procedure until all the batter is finished. Wipe the bottom of the skillet with oil between cooking the Atayif.

Bake in 350 °F oven for 10 minutes. Remove from oven and drop into cold syrup. Remove with a slotted spoon onto a platter.

VARIATION:
(1) Substitute 1 pound Ricotta cheese for the walnuts. Place a teaspoon into each round and proceed with the same directions.
(2) After pastry is filled and sealed, deep fry in vegetable oil. Drain and drop in cold syrup. Remove with slotted spoon.

Holy Bread

Urbaan

This bread is offered as Holy Communion in the Orthodox and Catholic churches in the Middle East. The bread is sometimes also served at Easter time for breakfast with cheese, olives and other breakfast foods.

1 tsp. sugar
½ cup lukewarm water
3 tsp. yeast
2 cups sugar
2 cups water (lukewarm)
1 cup milk (warm)

1 tsp. rosewater
1 tsp. mahlab, *(refer to page 13)*
9 cups flour
2 tsp. baking powder
    rosewater for brushing on after baking

Dissolve 1 teaspoon sugar in ½ cup water. Add yeast. Set aside for 5-10 minutes.

Meanwhile, dissolve the 2 cups of sugar in 2 cups water and 1 cup milk in a large bowl. Add rosewater, yeast mixture and mahlab. Gradually fold in flour and baking powder. Dough should be firm (the consistency of bread dough). Knead well.

Cover with plastic sheet then a tea towel. Leave to rest in a warm place for 1 hour. Knead again. Leave to rest another 30 minutes.

Divide dough into 12 balls. Roll out each into ½ inch thick rounds. Press lightly over each round with fingers. Then, press the teeth of a fork into the rounds to decorate. Cover and let rest for 20 minutes.

Bake in preheated 400°F oven for 15-20 minutes or until golden brown.

Remove from oven. Saturate a small cloth in rosewater and wipe thoroughly over Holy Bread.

Macaroni Pastry

5 cups flour
1 Tbsp. baking powder
1½ cups olive oil or good quality
    vegetable oil
1 cup sugar

1 tsp. anise seed powder
    (optional)
water
2 Syrup recipes (page 160)

Place flour and baking powder in a large bowl, add oil and rub with hands until mixed well. Add sugar and anise powder. Work well between hands. Add enough water to make the dough slightly softer than pie dough.

Pinch off from the dough an amount the size of a walnut. Place over a rough surface that has a design, such as a sieve, grater or a glass dish that is carved. Press the piece of dough flat onto the surface to make a design in the dough. Roll loosely into a thick finger shape and pinch once only to hold together, with the design on the outside.

Place on an ungreased baking sheet and bake at 375°F for 15-20 minutes to a light golden brown.

Dip into the prepared cold syrup. Remove with a slotted spoon.

VARIATION:
(1) Place ½ teaspoon crushed walnuts inside the piece of dough after the design is made, roll and bake.
(2) Deep fry fingers to a golden brown leaving out the filling.

Arabic Coffee

Quahwa Arabia

1 cup cold water
1 cardamon seed or
⅛ tsp. powder (optional)

1 tsp. sugar
2 Tbsp. Arabic or Turkish coffee
    (finely ground)

Place water in a small coffee pot or Raqui, a special Arabic coffee pot.

Crack the cardamon seed slightly, add to the water, add sugar and bring to boil. Remove from heat and add coffee. Return to heat and bring to boil 3 times; each time the coffee comes to boil, remove from heat, stir and return to heat to boil again. Let settle.

Spoon a little of the foam which has gathered on top of the coffee into each demitasse cup, then pour in coffee.

NOTE: Arabic coffee may be prepared sweeter or more bitter, depending on the individual taste.

Mint Tea

4 cups water
¼ cup fresh mint leaves *or*
2 Tbsp. dry
   sugar or honey

Bring water to boil in a saucepan, add mint leaves. Boil for 2-3 minutes. Strain and serve with sugar or honey to taste.

Anise Tea

3 cups water
1 Tbsp. whole anise seeds
   sugar or honey

Bring water to boil in a saucepan, add anise seeds and boil for 3-4 minutes. Strain and serve with sugar or honey to taste.

Spiced Tea

Ainar

This tea is usually served when celebrating the birth of a child. It is also excellent to treat stomach aches, omitting the walnuts.

5 cups water
¼ tsp. nutmeg
¼ tsp. anise seed powder
2 cinnamon sticks

¼ tsp. allspice
¼ cup walnut pieces
   sugar or honey

Combine water, nutmeg, anise seed powder, cinnamon sticks and allspice. Boil for 20 minutes. Strain.

Serve with walnut pieces added to each serving.

Add sugar or honey to taste.

Coffee-Grand Marnier Drink

1½ cups milk
  1 cup plain yogurt
  1 cup strong black coffee (cold)

4 Tbsp. Grand Marnier
1 Tbsp. lemon juice
4 Tbsp. berry sugar or icing sugar

Combine all ingredients in blender. Blend until smooth. Serve with ice cubes.

VARIATION:
Tia Maria or Kahlua may be substituted for Grand Marnier.

Yogurt-Pineapple Drink

1 cup plain yogurt
2 cups crushed pineapple (with juice)
1 ripe banana

1 cup milk
2 tsp. sugar or honey

Blend all ingredients in blender until smooth.

Pour over ice. Serve.

Yogurt Drink

½ glass plain yogurt
½ glass cold water
  ice cubes (optional)

Blend or whip yogurt and water together. Flavor with honey or sugar if desired.

Yogurt Shake

2 cups yogurt
1 cup fresh fruit (your flavor)
1 cup milk
  honey or syrup to taste

Blend all ingredients together.

Add honey or syrup to taste. Serve in tall glass.

INDEX

179

WHERE TO FIND INGREDIENTS

Arizona
Hajji Baba Middle Eastern
  Food
1513 East Apache
Tempe, AZ 85281

California
Levant International Food
  Co.
9421 Alondra Blvd.
Bellflower, CA 90706

Sunflower Grocery & Deli
20774 E. Arrow Hwy.
Covina, CA 91724

Eastern Market
852 Avocado Ave.
El Cajon, CA 92020

Fresno Deli
4627 Fresno St.
Fresno, CA 93726

M & J Market & Deli
12924 Vanowen St.
North Hollywood, CA
  91605

K & C Importing
2771 West Pico Blvd.
Los Angeles, CA 90006

Fairuz Middle Eastern
  Grocery
3306 N. Garey at Foothill
Pomona, CA 91767

International Groceries of
  San Diego
3548 Ashford St.
San Diego, CA 92111

Samiramis Importing Co.
2990 Mission St.
San Francisco, CA 94110

Middle East Food
26 Washington St.
Santa Clara, CA 95050

Sweis International
  Market
6809 Hazeltine Ave.
Van Nuys, CA 91405

Colorado
Middle East Grocery
2238 S. Colorado Blvd.
Denver, CO 80222

National Foods
1905 W. Mississippi
Denver, CO 80223

Connecticut
Shallah's Middle Eastern
  Importing Co.
290 White St.
Danbury, CT 06810

Florida
Damascus Imported
  Grocery
5721 Hollywood Blvd.
Hollywood, FL 33021

Eastern Star Bakery
440 S. W. 8th St.
Miami, FL 33130

Georgia
Middle East Baking Co.
4000-B Pleasantdale Rd.,
  N.E.
Atlanta, GA 30140

Middle Eastern Groceries
22-50 Cobb Parkway
Smyrna, GA 30080

Illinois
Holy Land Bakery &
  Grocery
4806-8 N. Kedzie Ave.
Chicago, IL 60625

Middle Eastern Bakery &
  Grocery
1512 W. Foster Ave.
Chicago, IL 60640

Maryland
Dokan Deli
7921 Old Georgetown Rd.
Bethesda, MD 20814

Yekta Deli
1488 Rockville Pike
Rockville, MD 20800

Massachusetts
Syrian Grocery
270 Shawmut Ave.
Boston, MA 02118

Lebanese Grocery
High Point Shopping
  Center
4640 Washington St. #4-3
Roslindale, MA 02131

Near East Baking Co.
5268 Washington
West Roxbury, MA 02132

181

New York

Oriental Grocery
170-172 Atlantic Ave.
Brooklyn, NY 11201

Sahadi Importing Co.
187 Atlantic Ave.
Brooklyn, NY 11201

Nadar Import
One East 28th St.
New York, NY 10016

Sunflower Store
97-22 Queens Blvd.
Rego Park, NY 11374

Nablus Grocery
456 S. Broadway
Yonkers, NY 10705

North Carolina

NUR, Inc.
223 Avent Ferry Road
  #108
Raleigh, NC 27606

Ohio

University Market
300 E. Exchange
Akron, OH 44304

Middle East Foods
19-57 West 25th St.
Cleveland, OH 44113

Sinbad Food Imports
2620 N. High St.
Columbus, OH 43202

Oklahoma

Mediterranean Imports &
  Health Foods
36-27 North MacArthur
Oklahoma City, OK 73122

Michigan

The Arabic Town
16511 Woodward
Highland Park, MI 48203

Minnesota

Ali Baba Bakery
2507 Central Ave., N.E.
Minneapolis, MN 55418

Missouri

Campus Eastern Foods
408 Locust Street #B
Columbia, MO 65201

New Jersey

Fattal's Syrian Bakery
977 Main St.
Paterson, NJ 07503

Nouri's Syrian Bakery &
  Grocery
983-989 Main St.
Paterson, NJ 07503

Al-Khayam
7723 Bergenline Ave.
North Bergen, NJ 07047

Pennsylvania

Makhoul Corner Store
448 N. 2nd St.
Allentown, PA 18102

Bitar's
947 Federal St.
Philadelphia, PA 19147

Salim's Middle Eastern
  Food Store
47-05 Center Ave.
Pittsburgh, PA 15213

Texas

Rana Food Store
1623 West Arkansas Lane
Arlington, TX 76013

Phoenicia Bakery & Deli
2912 S. Lamar
Austin, TX 78704

Worldwide Foods
2203 Greenville Ave.
Dallas, TX 75206

Droubi's Bakery &
  Grocery
7333 Hillcroft
Houston, TX 77081

Jerusalem Bakery &
  Grocery
201 E. Main
Richardson, TX 75081

Virginia

Mediterranean Bakery
374 S. Picket St.
Alexandria, VA 22304

Halalco
108 E. Fairfax St.
Falls Church, VA 22046

NOTES

NOTES

NOTES

NOTES

NOTES

NOTES

NOTES

NOTES